The Final Farewell

Exploring Post-Death Treatment Options

Bridget Marie

Table of Contents

INTRODUCTION 1

CHAPTER 1: 100% MORTALITY RATE 5

MISCONCEPTIONS AND ATTITUDES TOWARD DEATH 5
  Denial and Avoidance 6
  Taboos and Stigma 6
  Fear of Loss of Control 6
  Cultural and Religious Beliefs 7
WHY POST-DEATH PLANNING MATTERS 7
HONORING END-OF-LIFE WISHES TOGETHER 10
  Preserving Individual Autonomy 10
  Alleviating Family Conflict 11
  Ensuring Lasting Peace of Mind 11
THE ROLE OF EDUCATION: UNDERSTANDING POST-DEATH TREATMENT
OPTIONS 12
  Exploring the Options 12
  Considerations and Reflections 13
  Embracing Choice and Diversity 13
  Importance of Informed Decision-Making 14
  Empowering Choices 16

CHAPTER 2: BURIAL 19

THE DOMINANCE OF BURIAL 19
  Tradition: Keeping the Flame Alive 19
  Religious Roots: Divine Guidance 20
  Evolution of Religious Attitudes Toward Burial 20
CHOOSING BETWEEN CASKETS AND COFFINS 21
  Navigating Design and Cost Considerations 22
FUNERAL PROCEDURES 24
  Preparing for Farewell 24
  The Art of Restoration 25

Balancing Tradition and Ethics 25
Embracing Alternative Practices 26
THE SIGNIFICANCE OF EMBALMING 26
Legal Considerations and Natural Benefits 26
Environmental Impact and Alternatives 27
DECOMPOSITION AND ENVIRONMENTAL IMPACT 27
Natural Decomposition 27
Effects of Burial Conditions on Decay Rate 28
Timeline of Decomposition in a Casket 28
ENVIRONMENTAL CONCERNS AND ETHICAL CONSIDERATIONS 29
Toxicity and Environmental Implications 30
Formaldehyde Usage and Disposal 30
DISPOSAL OF BODY FLUIDS 31
Impact on Wastewater Treatment 31
Public Health Implications 32
Mitigation Measures 32
REFLECTING ON BURIAL PRACTICES 33

CHAPTER 3: CREMATION 35

UNDERSTANDING CREMATION: A JOURNEY INTO TRANSFORMATION .. 35
Defining Cremation: From Body to Ashes 36
The Mechanics of Cremation 37
Cultural and Religious Perspectives on Cremation 38
FACTORS INFLUENCING THE RISE OF CREMATION 40
Cost-Effectiveness and Financial Flexibility 40
Addressing Space Constraints and Eco-Consciousness 41
Streamlining End-of-Life Arrangements 42
NAVIGATING THE CREMATION PROCESS: REGULATIONS AND
PRACTICALITIES 43
Waiting Periods and Organ Donation Procedures 43
Removal of Items Before Cremation Procedures 44
Debunking Myths 45

CHAPTER 4: WHOLE BODY DONATION TO SCIENCE 49

UNDERSTANDING THE GIFT 49
Importance in Medical Education and Research 51
HOW DOES THE PROCESS WORK? 53
EXPLORING PERSONAL VALUES AND ETHICAL CONSIDERATIONS 54

Reflecting on Personal Beliefs..54
Ethical Reflection 55
Seeking Guidance 55
DISCUSSING INTENTIONS WITH LOVED ONES.....................................56
Importance of Open Dialogue 57
Addressing Concerns...57
Facilitating Understanding 57
Initiating the Conversation 58
Sharing Your Intentions 58
Listening to Their Thoughts 58
Creating a Plan Together...59
RESOURCES AND SUPPORT FOR THOSE CONSIDERING BODY DONATION
....59
Accessing Information 59
Support Networks...60
Professional Guidance 62
POST-DONATION ARRANGEMENTS 62
Transporting the Body to the Facility 63
Understanding the Facility's Policies 63
Ensuring Eventual Disposition of Remains........................64

CHAPTER 5: GREEN (OR NATURAL) BURIAL 67

UNDERSTANDING GREEN BURIAL 69
A Natural Return to the Earth..70
The Depth of Burial and Its Implications........................71
Environmental Benefits and Growing Popularity 72
KEY FEATURES OF GREEN BURIAL 73
Decomposition Process: Natural Decay Without
Embalming..73
Types of Caskets and Shrouds: Biodegradable Materials 74
The Innovative Option: Mushroom Burial Suit by Coeio..76
Limitations on Memorial Markers in Green Burial
Cemeteries...77
AVAILABILITY AND PRACTICAL CONSIDERATIONS 79
Availability of Green Burial Cemeteries Across the United
States...79
Duration of Decomposition Based on Soil Type, Oxygen,
and Moisture 80

Cultural Acceptance of Green Burial Within the Catholic Community 82

CHAPTER 6: AQUAMATION 85

HISTORICAL BACKGROUND 85
Origins of Aquamation 85
Early Uses in Agriculture and Laboratory Settings 87
Aquamation Technology Evolution 88
THE AQUAMATION PROCESS 89
COMMERCIAL ADOPTION AND REGULATORY LANDSCAPE 91
First Commercial Aquamation at Albany Medical College 91
Cost-Effective Animal Commercial Use 92
Minnesota's Pioneering Approval of Aquamation 94
Variations in State Regulations 95
ENVIRONMENTAL IMPACT AND BENEFITS 96
Aquamation vs. Traditional Cremation and Burial 96

CHAPTER 7: TREE POD BURIAL 99

OVERVIEW OF THE CONCEPT OF TREE POD BURIALS 99
The Birth of an Eco-Friendly Legacy: Capsula Mundi 100
Visualizing the Burial Process 101
Environmental Benefits and Symbolism 102
CURRENT OPTIONS 103
Global Capsula Mundi Limitations 103
Eco-Friendly Memorial Growth 105
Choosing the Right Tree 106
PRACTICAL CONSIDERATIONS AND LOGISTICS 107
Cost Analysis 107
Options for Acquiring Burial Pods and Trees 109
Legal Aspect 110

CHAPTER 8: TERRAMATION 113

UNDERSTANDING TERRAMATION 113
THE PROCESS OF TERRAMATION 115
Sealed Chamber Composting 115
Duration and Stages 116
ENVIRONMENTAL BENEFITS 117

ETHICAL AND RELIGIOUS PERSPECTIVES 119
   Examination of Ethical Implications 119
   Perspectives From Different Religious Traditions 120
   Addressing Concerns and Encouraging Dialogue 121
LEGAL ACCEPTANCE 122
   Current Legal Status 122
   Growing Support and Legislative Progress 122
   Regional Availability 123
COST ANALYSIS 123
EMOTIONAL AND SYMBOLIC SIGNIFICANCE OF TERRAMATION 125
   Personal Connection to the Earth 125
   Creation of Memorial Gardens 126
   Family Involvement and Commemoration 126
PROSPECTS FOR THE FUTURE 127

CHAPTER 9: BURIAL AT SEA **129**

DEATH AS LIFE'S CULMINATION 129
   The True Story of Lois Woodburn 130
   The Ceremony 130
HISTORICAL AND PRACTICAL ASPECTS 132
   Historical Context of Burial at Sea 132
   Modern Practices and Regulations Governing Burial at Sea 132
EXPLORING THE TRADITIONS OF BURIAL AT SEA 134
   For Civilians 134
   For Military Veterans 136
REASONS FOR CHOOSING BURIAL AT SEA 137
   Environmental Benefits and Considerations 137
   Financial Considerations Compared to Traditional Burials 138
   Personal Connection to the Ocean 138
MARITIME TRIBUTES 139

CHAPTER 10: THE FUTURE - ICE BURIAL (PROMESSION) **143**

THE ALLURE OF FUTURISTIC BODY DISPOSITION METHODS 143
   Introducing Promession: A Novel Approach to Body Reduction 144
DEVELOPMENT BY SWEDISH BIOLOGIST SUSANNE WIIGH-MÄSAK 145

Liquidation of Promessa Company in 2015 146
Wiigh-Mäsak's Legacy and Dedication to Promession .. 147
THE PROMESSION PROCESS UNVEILED 147
Cryogenic Freezing Chamber Initiation......................... 148
Liquid Nitrogen Application and Crystallization of Body
Cells 148
Mechanically Induced Vibration for Cell Disintegration 148
Sublimation.. 149
Resulting Powder.. 149
HANDLING AND PREPARATION OF REMAINS 150
Removal of Metals Through Magnetic or Sieving Processes
.... 150
Containment in Biodegradable Materials 151
Ethical and Environmental Considerations.................... 152
LEGAL AND CULTURAL ACCEPTANCE.. 152
Current Legal Status in Sweden, the U.K., and South Korea
.... 152
Societal Perceptions and Cultural Implications 154
REFLECTING ON THE POTENTIAL OF PROMESSION 156
Future of Body Disposition Technology 157

CONCLUSION 159

BONUS MATERIAL: WHAT CAN BE DONE WITH THE ASHES?
.... 163

UNIQUE MEMORIALIZATION IDEAS FOR ASHES.............................. 163
Custom Urns 163
INCORPORATING ASHES INTO CREATIVE EXPRESSIONS 165
Artistic Tributes 165
UNCONVENTIONAL CELEBRATIONS OF LIFE 166
Spectacular Farewells: Creating Vibrant Firework Displays
With Ashes.. 166
Futuristic Farewells: Sending Ashes Into Space as a Cosmic
Tribute 167
Environmental Consciousness: Transforming Ashes Into
Artificial Coral Reefs 167

ABOUT THE AUTHOR 169

REFERENCES 171

Introduction

If you're holding this book, you've probably faced the daunting task of deciding what to do with a loved one's remains after their passing. Perhaps they never made their wishes known, leaving you to grapple with this burden amid your grief. Or maybe you're thinking about your own end-of-life plans and realizing the importance of relieving your loved ones from this weight when your time comes.

Losing a loved one is an experience that shakes us to our core, leaving us with profound grief and a multitude of decisions to make. It's a burden that can weigh heavily on us during an already overwhelming time. By confronting the realities of mortality and planning for our final farewell with intention and compassion, we can honor our loved ones' memories while also leaving behind a legacy of love and preparedness.

My name is Bridget Marie and I understand the pain and uncertainty that accompany these decisions. It's a topic often shrouded in discomfort, avoided at all costs until it can no longer be ignored. However, avoiding it won't make it disappear. The truth is, each one of us will reach the end of our journey eventually, some sooner than expected. It's time to confront this reality directly.

Undoubtedly, despite the fact that discussing end-of-life matters is uncomfortable, you need to confront these realities and empower yourself with knowledge. By reading The *Final Farewell: Exploring Post-Death Treatment Options*, you'll acquire insight into the different ways to handle remains, allowing you to make informed decisions that align with your values and preferences.

This book isn't about dwelling on morbidity; it's about empowerment. It aims to equip you with knowledge so you can make informed decisions about post-death treatment options. By making these decisions, you not only ease the burden on your loved ones but also ensure that your final wishes are respected.

In the following chapters, we'll delve into the various types of body disposition available, from traditional burials to eco-friendly alternatives such as green burials and aquamation. Each option has its considerations, ecological impact, and cost. I'll discuss the environmental consequences of each option, helping you make decisions that not only honor your loved ones but also minimize your impact on the planet.

Before we delve into the specifics, it's crucial to acknowledge a fundamental truth: death is a universal experience. Regardless of our age, background, or beliefs, we all share the certainty of our mortality. And, while it's natural to avoid discussions about death, doing so only perpetuates the stigma and fear surrounding this inevitable fact of life.

Therefore, let's embrace the opportunity to have open, honest conversations about our end-of-life wishes. Whether you're planning for yourself or supporting a grieving loved one, having these discussions can offer clarity and peace of mind during a difficult time.

Although burial is the most common yet often the most expensive option, it is not the only option, nor is it always the most environmentally responsible. There are several popular options for post-death treatment to choose from. I'll guide you through each option, discussing their pros, cons, and environmental impact. These alternatives offer unique ways to honor loved ones while also embracing innovative approaches to end-of-life care. By delving into the diverse array of post-death treatment methods, we can make choices that are consistent with our values and leave a positive impact on the world around us.

One such option is tree pod burial, which involves planting a tree alongside a buried pod containing the remains of the deceased. This eco-friendly approach allows for a beautiful symbiosis between the deceased and nature, as the pod decomposes over time, nourishing the growing tree.

Terramation, also known as human composting, is another environmentally friendly option. Unlike traditional burial or cremation, this approach gently transforms the body into soil, resembling the natural process of composting. With the use of a charcoal filter, this approach effectively eliminates odors, making it a dignified and eco-friendly alternative.

For those with a connection to the sea, burial at sea is a poignant farewell, allowing the deceased to rest eternally in the waters they once navigated. It's a poetic way to honor a life spent on the waves.

The Final Farewell also glimpses into the future with the concept of ice burial or promession. This innovative method, currently in use in a few countries, uses freeze-drying technology to convert the body to powder, offering an alternative to traditional cremation with potentially lower environmental impact.

Furthermore, this book addresses common questions and concerns about post-death treatment methods, providing practical guidance and resources to assist you throughout the decision-making process. Whether you're researching burial traditions, considering the environmental impact of different methods, or simply looking for advice on how to broach this subject with your loved ones, this book offers a safe space for learning and reflection.

I urge readers to seize the opportunity for discussion and exploration. I hope to alleviate some of the burden of making end-of-life decisions by providing insight and understanding. By arming ourselves with proper knowledge and opening up discourse about these difficult matters, we can ensure that our end-of-life wishes are understood and respected, easing the burden on our loved ones during their period of grief.

So, if you have ever felt uncertain about what to do with a loved one's remains or want to ensure your own wishes are honored, I invite you to join me on this journey. Let's explore the options together and pave the way for a more thoughtful and compassionate approach to death and dying.

Chapter 1:

100% Mortality Rate

This chapter addresses the undeniable truth that all living beings will inevitably die, laying the groundwork for a discussion about the need for understanding mortality and making plans for post-death arrangements. We will discuss common misconceptions about death, the importance of open communication within families, and the role of education in raising awareness about different options for post-death treatment.

Misconceptions and Attitudes Toward Death

Death is often a topic shrouded in misconceptions and avoidance in many cultures around the world. Addressing these misconceptions and attitudes toward death is crucial for promoting a better knowledge of mortality and end-of-life planning.

Denial and Avoidance

One of the most prevalent attitudes toward death is denial and avoidance. Many people are uncomfortable confronting their death, and they might avoid discussing or making plans for end-of-life care and arrangements altogether. This attitude stems from a fear of the unknown and the natural human instinct to cling to life. However, by avoiding the topic of death, individuals might miss out on important opportunities to express their wishes and ensure a peaceful transition for themselves and their loved ones.

Taboos and Stigma

In some cultures, death is surrounded by taboos and stigmas, making it a topic that is not often discussed openly. This might cause feelings of loneliness and humiliation among persons dealing with bereavement or end-of-life decisions. Breaking down these taboos and stigmas is crucial in building a more helpful and understanding atmosphere for people dealing with death and loss. Encouraging open conversations about death can help normalize the experience and provide much-needed support to those going through the end-of-life process.

Fear of Loss of Control

Another common misconception surrounding death is the fear of losing control. Many people are concerned that planning for their own death might speed up the process or reduce their current quality of life. However, the truth is quite the reverse. Taking control of end-of-life decisions, such as advance care planning and pre-arranging funeral or burial arrangements, can bring a sense of empowerment and peace of mind. Individuals who outline their desires in advance can ensure that their values and preferences are honored while also easing the load on their loved ones during an already difficult time.

Cultural and Religious Beliefs

Cultural and religious beliefs also play a significant role in shaping attitudes toward death (Lang et al., 2022). Different cultures and faith traditions have unique rituals and customs surrounding death and mourning, which can influence how people approach end-of-life planning. Understanding and respecting these cultural and religious beliefs is important for delivering culturally sensitive care and support to individuals experiencing death and grief. By acknowledging and honoring diverse perspectives on death, we can build a more inclusive and compassionate society that helps individuals of all backgrounds in their end-of-life journey.

Why Post-Death Planning Matters

Post-death planning is not just for the elderly or those with terminal illnesses; it is an important aspect of life that everyone should consider. But why should it matter?

Let me share a personal story that sheds light on this important question.

Some time ago, I found myself engaged in a conversation about my writing project, namely the many alternatives for body disposition after death. As I explained my passion for this subject, I was met with a skeptical response.

"What exactly are you writing about?" my friend asked, curiosity tinged with disbelief in her tone.

"I'm exploring the many ways people can choose to dispose of their bodies after death," I replied.

"But why?" she persisted.

I paused, surprised by the question. Why indeed? It was a moment of reflection that prompted me to articulate my belief in the importance of post-death planning. "Because," I began, "it's a decision that everyone should make in their lifetime. It's a personal decision that shouldn't burden bereaved family members."

She shrugged dismissively. "Why should I worry about what happens to me after I die? That's their problem!" she said, referring to her family.

I was momentarily at a loss for words. But in that moment of silence, my mind raced with thoughts. It doesn't have to be this way. Post-death decisions should not be viewed as a burden to be passed on to family and friends in their time of grief. Instead, it should be a chance for honest, loving communication among family members, bringing them closer together.

This interaction reaffirmed my belief that post-death planning is important. It's more than just making practical arrangements; it's about respecting the deceased's wishes and ideals. It's about easing the burden on grieving loved ones and ensuring that a person's final wishes are respected.

Here we have another common misconception that often surrounds post-death planning: the belief that it's solely the responsibility of grieving family members. However, this assertion is completely inaccurate. Individuals who fail to plan ahead risk leaving their loved ones with difficult options to make during an already trying time.

That's why it's essential to have these conversations early and often. Discussing post-death arrangements isn't morbid; it's pragmatic. It's about taking control of our own destiny and making sure that our wishes are heard and respected.

By learning about the numerous alternatives for post-death disposition, we empower ourselves to make informed decisions that are consistent with our values and preferences. Post-death planning is a topic that deserves our attention and consideration, and by facing it head-on, we can ensure that our final wishes are carried out and our loved ones are spared needless stress and confusion.

Honoring End-of-Life Wishes Together

Open communication within families—taking place before the inevitable occurrence of death—ensures that individuals can have their wishes honored and their legacy respected (Caregiving.com, 2023). It serves as a basis for developing understanding, empathy, and solidarity during the difficult time of grieving. Let's delve deeper into why this is important and how it can positively impact the post-death process.

Preserving Individual Autonomy

Every individual's life journey is as unique as a fingerprint, and so is the journey of their end-of-life plans. By initiating open conversations with close friends and family members about their preferences and desires regarding their final moments, individuals can assert their autonomy and ensure that their wishes are fulfilled with dignity. Encouraging honest discussion in a calm and supportive environment allows each family member to voice their opinions and concerns without fear of being judged.

Once these discussions have taken place, it's crucial to document preferences in a legally binding document, such as a will, advance directive, or chosen healthcare proxy. This ensures a clear road map for decision-making in the event of incapacitation or death, bringing peace of mind to everyone involved.

Alleviating Family Conflict

Navigating end-of-life decisions without clear directives from the deceased can strain familial relationships, resulting in arguments and unresolved conflicts. However, open communication about this can help families avoid problems and respect their loved one's legacy harmoniously. Unified by a shared understanding of the deceased's preferences, families find peace and support in fulfilling these wishes together (Keeley, 2017). Moreover, respecting diverse beliefs and traditions within the family promotes inclusivity and understanding, easing the decision-making process during a time of profound loss.

Ensuring Lasting Peace of Mind

Facing one's own mortality can be a daunting prospect but, by ensuring that one's wishes are understood and respected, individuals can find solace and peace in their final days. Engaging in open discussions with those who are dear to us regarding end-of-life care, funeral plans, and any cultural or religious preferences can help ease the strain on family members and ensure a dignified farewell. Additionally, accepting these conversations as an opportunity to celebrate life and legacy develops a sense of connection and facilitates the sharing of cherished memories and reflections, resulting in a meaningful tribute to a life well-lived.

The Role of Education: Understanding Post-Death Treatment Options

When it comes to post-death treatment options, many people are unaware of the array of choices available to them. However, understanding these options is necessary for making informed decisions that align with personal values and preferences.

Exploring the Options

Exploring the options available for post-death planning is similar to starting an excursion of self-discovery and introspection. It's a process that encourages people to consider not only their own mortality but also the legacy they want to leave behind. Traditionally, the choices of burial or cremation have been deeply ingrained in cultural practices worldwide, offering distinct rituals and symbolism to honor the deceased.

However, in recent years, there has been a noticeable shift toward exploring alternative solutions that are more closely aligned with changing cultural values and environmental awareness. This transition reflects a broader cultural awakening to the interconnectedness of human life and the natural world. As people become more aware of their environmental impact, they seek post-death traditions that resonate with their commitment to environmental sustainability.

Considerations and Reflections

Choosing a post-death alternative isn't just about logistics; it's a deeply personal decision based on your values, beliefs, and environmental concerns. Each option has its own set of considerations, requiring you to reflect thoroughly on what is most important to you.

Making such a significant decision can feel overwhelming, but you don't have to navigate it alone. Reach out to loved ones, religious or spiritual advisors, and professionals who specialize in end-of-life planning. Their insights and perspectives can be very helpful as you weigh your options. Discussing your thoughts and concerns openly can also provide emotional support during this reflective time.

Take the time to think about the aspects of life that matter the most to you. What legacy do you hope to leave behind? How do you imagine your final resting place? Consider how each option aligns with your values, beliefs, and vision for the future. Remember, there is no right or wrong choice; what matters is that the decision feels authentic and meaningful to you.

Embracing Choice and Diversity

When it comes to post-mortem planning, there is no one-size-fits-all solution. Instead, it is a vibrant tapestry of alternatives, each expressing an individual's unique values and views. This diversity is not only acceptable but also something to be celebrated.

Consider it an adventure in which you can choose your own path; one that is unique to you. Whether you choose a traditional burial, cremation, or natural interment, or you opt to donate your body to science, the goal is to make decisions that reflect who you are and what you believe in. It's about embracing the richness of your identity and leaving a lasting imprint on the world, even after you've bid your final farewell. Each decision you make is like a brushstroke on the canvas of your life, representing your values, beliefs, and goals.

So, don't feel restricted by norms or conventions. Instead, revel in the freedom of doing things your own way. Whether you envision a serene resting place in nature or aspire to contribute to scientific advancement, the power lies in your hands to shape your legacy.

Importance of Informed Decision-Making

The importance of informed decision-making in post-death planning cannot be overstated. By understanding the consequences of each choice and arming oneself with knowledge, individuals can navigate this delicate process with confidence, dignity, and grace.

Each choice in post-death planning has its own set of practical and emotional consequences. For example, opting for a natural burial aligns with strong environmental convictions, as it minimizes the use of resources and protects natural habitats. Cremation, on the other hand, can appeal to people for personal or cultural reasons, such as a belief in the soul's liberation from the physical body or adherence to religious customs.

Understanding these ramifications allows individuals to weigh the pros and cons of each option against their own values and beliefs. It enables them to make decisions that not only feel right on the surface but also speak to them on a deeper, more meaningful level. This congruence of personal beliefs with end-of-life decisions can bring a sense of calm and contentment, knowing that one's final wishes are being honored in a meaningful way.

In addition, individuals who educate themselves about post-death options gain control over their end-of-life experience. They go from a state of uncertainty and passiveness to one of clarity and agency. Armed with knowledge, people can confidently express their preferences and desires to their close friends and relatives and make choices that feel authentic to who they are.

Overall, informed decision-making extends beyond the individual. It can have a ripple effect, influencing and inspiring others to consider their own end-of-life preferences and have meaningful conversations with their families and dear ones. By setting a good example, individuals can promote a culture of openness, honesty, and acceptance surrounding death and dying, a culture in which post-death planning is viewed as a normal and important part of life rather than something unpleasant.

Empowering Choices

Each person's life journey is unique, and their death journey should be as well. Individuals can have the opportunity to personalize their end-of-life choices by understanding the many options available.

The goal is not to persuade people to adopt a specific disposition but rather to provide them with the knowledge and resources they need to make decisions that resonate with their innermost selves. Regardless of the post-death treatment method, the goal is to ensure that the chosen option accurately reflects the individual's preferences.

Furthermore, empowering decisions in post-death planning promotes a sense of agency and control over one's fate. In a world where death is often viewed negatively, taking proactive measures toward end-of-life planning can be very empowering. It allows individuals to reclaim control of their narratives, embracing death as a natural part of life rather than something to be feared or avoided.

Ultimately, the true measure of success in post-death planning lies not in the method chosen but in the sense of peace and comfort it brings to the individual. Whether it's knowing that one will return to the earth in a natural burial or taking comfort in the concept of having one's ashes dispersed in a cherished place, the importance lies in honoring the individual's wishes with dignity and respect.

In essence, empowering choices in post-death treatment options reaffirms the intrinsic dignity and worth of every individual. It is a testament to the profound value of personal autonomy and the right to choose one's own path, even in life's final phase.

As we conclude our exploration of the universal truth of mortality, it becomes evident that confronting this reality is the first step toward thoughtful end-of-life planning. Moving on from acknowledging our mortality, we dig into the timeless ritual of burial, a pillar of human society that provides comfort and continuity in the face of loss. In the following chapter, we will explore the cultural, religious, and personal significance of burial, shedding light on the timeless practices that have shaped our understanding of life, death, and legacy.

Chapter 2:

Burial

Embarking on the exploration of burial practices, this chapter sheds light on why this age-old tradition remains one of the predominant choices for post-death preparations. From the difficult process of choosing between coffins and caskets to the environmental impact of embalming, we uncover the complexities and considerations surrounding burial. Delving deeper, we confront ethical dilemmas and environmental concerns, urging thoughtful reflection and informed decision-making in navigating the end-of-life process.

The Dominance of Burial

Burial has stood the test of time as the go-to choice for laying our loved ones to rest, but what makes it such a prevalent practice? Let's look at the reasons why burial is the most popular post-death approach.

Tradition: Keeping the Flame Alive

Burial's popularity stems from its strong link to tradition. Since ancient times, societies all across the world have entrusted their deceased to the earth, regarding burial as a dignified act of honoring and preserving the memory of people who have died. This age-old habit, passed down from generation to generation, is an essential component of our cultural identity and collective heritage.

Religious Roots: Divine Guidance

Religion has a significant influence on burial preferences. Across numerous faiths and beliefs, burial is often regarded as the preferable manner of body disposition, owing to the influence of religious principles and sacred teachings. (American Heritage, 2021). For many, the act of burying the departed is not just a matter of tradition but a sacred duty that symbolizes a spiritual journey into the hereafter. These religious mandates infuse burial with profound meaning, thus shaping our attitudes and practices toward death.

In essence, burial's domination stems from a harmonic blend of tradition and religious reverence, which connects the threads of cultural legacy and spiritual devotion. It's this timeless union that continues to uphold burial as a cherished and enduring tradition in our society.

Evolution of Religious Attitudes Toward Burial

Over the centuries, religious beliefs have shaped how we handle the deceased, and burial practices have evolved alongside these beliefs. While burial has long been the preferred method for laying loved ones to rest, religious sentiments regarding it have shifted throughout history.

In the past, religious doctrines often dictated strict guidelines for burial, prohibiting alternatives like cremation. However, as cultures evolve and perceptions vary, religious interpretations become more adaptable. For example, what was previously considered taboo may now be acceptable in some contexts, such as cremation under certain conditions.

This evolution reflects not only changes in religious doctrine but also broader shifts in cultural norms and values. As we continue to navigate these changes, the dominance of burial remains deeply linked to tradition while also adjusting to accommodate the demands and values of modern society.

Choosing Between Caskets and Coffins

When the time comes to bid farewell to a loved one, the journey usually begins with a visit to the local funeral home. This important time marks the beginning of a sensitive process in which decisions regarding the deceased's final resting place must be made. At the center of these decisions is a choice between two famous vessels: the casket and the coffin.

Consider this: you find yourself standing in the serene atmosphere of the funeral home, surrounded by rows of perfectly built caskets and coffins. Each promises a dignified final resting place for your beloved. But how do you decide between them? What sets them apart?

Let's start by understanding the fundamental differences between caskets and coffins (Schilling Funeral Home, 2021). While these terms are often used interchangeably, they have distinct characteristics catering to different preferences and needs.

Navigating Design and Cost Considerations

Coffins, with their ageless design, evoke memories of a bygone period. They have six sides and a characteristic tapering design that is wider at the shoulders but narrower at the head and foot. This timeless design exudes simplicity and elegance while instilling a feeling of tradition and heritage. Coffins are popular for their rustic charm and for individuals who prefer a more traditional burial experience.

Caskets, on the other hand, have a more streamlined and modern appearance. They are rectangular in design and have four sides, providing a modern appearance that many people enjoy. Caskets are frequently decorated with lengthy rails along the edges, which provide a convenient solution for pallbearers during the funeral procession. With their refined appearance and customizable features, caskets are favored by those seeking a more personalized touch to honor their loved one's memory.

Aside from design differences, another important issue to consider is pricing. Coffins are generally less expensive than caskets with their simpler construction and rustic look. This makes them an appealing option for budget-conscious households. However, caskets (with their sleek design and customizable features) can command a higher price tag, ranging from moderate to exorbitant costs depending on materials and craftsmanship.

As families struggle with these decisions, they find themselves walking a fine line between tradition and practicality. While the desire to preserve long-standing traditions might lead to a traditional coffin, practical considerations like money restrictions or environmental concerns might lead to a more modern casket. Ultimately, the chosen vessel serves as a poignant tribute, reflecting not only the individual's life but also the values and beliefs held dear by those left behind.

In navigating this aspect of the burial process, families are tasked with not only honoring the wishes of the departed but also finding comfort in the meaningful choices made to commemorate their legacy. Through collaboration with funeral home professionals and thoughtful consideration of options, the path toward saying goodbye becomes a heartfelt tribute to a life fulfilled.

Funeral Procedures

When someone dear to you passes away, their final journey begins with the tender care of the funeral staff (including the funeral director, mortician, and embalmer), who undertake the solemn responsibility of preparing the corpse for burial. This delicate process includes a series of painstaking measures meant to provide dignity and respect for the deceased.

Preparing for Farewell

In cases where the deceased has generously chosen to be an organ donor, the process is handled with great care. The donor is quickly transferred to a hospital operating room, where qualified medical personnel perform surgery to extract the organs for transplantation, thus assuring their viability for others in need (UNOS, n.d.).

Following organ removal, the donor is respectfully conveyed to the funeral home. With profound reverence, the mortician or embalmer carefully attends to the intricate details of the human body, establishing a delicate balance between respect for the departed and pragmatic necessities. The Organ Procurement Organization (OPO) works with the funeral director to fulfill the donor's and their family's funeral arrangements. In the peaceful confines of the funeral home, the embalmer begins their sacred task by carefully washing and scrubbing the body, a gesture full of reverence. This initial act, symbolic of purification, seeks to restore the departed to a state of peace before their journey into eternity.

Embalming the body is a practice steeped in tradition yet fraught with controversy. This technique involves the injecting of preservation fluids into the vascular system, which effectively slows the natural decay process. While some see embalming as a way to pay tribute to the deceased, others dispute its usefulness and environmental impact. Despite these debates, embalming remains a prevalent practice in many cultures, symbolizing the preservation of one's legacy for posterity.

The Art of Restoration

In addition to washing the body and embalming, morticians or funeral directors often practice or oversee the delicate art of restoration. This includes cosmetic procedures to restore the deceased's appearance to its natural state. Morticians approach restoration with a blend of skill and compassion, whether it is healing trauma caused by accidents or disease or just improving features for a peaceful rest. Through their meticulous efforts, they endeavor to present the departed in a manner that brings solace to grieving loved ones.

Balancing Tradition and Ethics

Funeral home procedures for embalming, rooted in tradition, raise ethical concerns about consent and environmental damage. Embalming, which uses chemical preservatives, raises worries about environmental impact and potential health dangers. Funeral directors handle these issues with compassion, aiming to maintain cultural traditions and ethical norms in their work.

Embracing Alternative Practices

Amid evolving attitudes towards death and burial, some individuals opt for alternative approaches that differ from traditional mortician procedures. From eco-friendly burial methods to natural decomposition processes, these alternatives offer new avenues for honoring the deceased while reducing environmental impact. While diverging from conventional norms, these practices highlight the importance of choice and personalization in end-of-life arrangements.

The Significance of Embalming

Legal Considerations and Natural Benefits

Contrary to popular belief, embalming isn't legally required. While it's often associated with preserving the body for viewing, its legal necessity varies widely. Furthermore, despite its widespread use, embalming has no inherent health benefits and only delays the natural decomposition process for a brief period.

Environmental Impact and Alternatives

Despite its seemingly harmless function, embalming has serious environmental consequences. The chemicals utilized, such as formaldehyde, are hazardous to both the environment and individuals who handle them. In the United States alone, about 20 million liters (roughly 5.3 million gallons) of embalming fluid are used every year (Tan, 2021). As people become more aware of environmental issues, eco-friendly embalming fluids and chemical-free preservation procedures are gaining popularity (Mobility Foresights, 2024). Exploring these alternatives not only reduces environmental harm but also offers families more sustainable and conscientious choices in honoring their loved ones.

Decomposition and Environmental Impact

Natural Decomposition

When a body is buried, it begins its natural decomposition, impacted by various factors that affect the rate at which it breaks down. Among these factors, burial conditions play a crucial role, with the choice of container having a major impact on the decomposition process (Death Curious, 2023).

Effects of Burial Conditions on Decay Rate

The environment in which a body is interred determines the rate at which it decomposes. Airtight and moisture-tight containers, which are commonly employed in traditional burial methods, produce an environment that slows down the natural decay process. By sealing off the body from external elements such as air and moisture, these containers inhibit the growth of microorganisms responsible for decomposition. As a result, the body remains preserved for a longer period, altering the timeline of decay.

Traditionally, the use of coffins and caskets has been synonymous with burial, with many opting for these sealed containers to protect the body from the atmosphere. While this might seem like a dignified way to lay the deceased to rest, it inadvertently prolongs the decomposition process and contributes to environmental concerns.

Timeline of Decomposition in a Casket

In a casket buried underground, the absence of oxygen slows down the decay of organic matter within the body. Typically, decomposition under such conditions takes place over a prolonged period, ranging from 10 to 15 years. However, the timescale may differ depending on several circumstances, including the type of casket used, burial depth, soil composition, and weather conditions.

Materials utilized in modern caskets, such as metal or hardwood, further limit the body's natural disintegration by forming a barrier that hinders microbial activity. As a result, even years after burial, the deceased's remains (such as bones, teeth and hair) might still be identifiable within the casket.

While some might view this extended preservation as a way to honor the deceased, it poses ethical and environmental concerns. The use of nonbiodegradable materials in caskets not only impedes the return of organic matter to the earth but also contributes to resource depletion and pollution.

Environmental Concerns and Ethical Considerations

In our quest to understand burial practices, it's essential to explore the environmental consequences and ethical dilemmas that come with embalming. We will now explore the profound impact of embalming chemicals on our ecosystem, as well as the ethical considerations surrounding their use and disposal.

When we bid farewell to a loved one through burial, we don't often consider the hidden costs beneath the surface. Embalming, which aims to preserve the body, uses a variety of chemicals, including the renowned formaldehyde (Georgia, n.d.). While this process might temporarily stall decomposition, the environmental repercussions are far-reaching and significant.

Toxicity and Environmental Implications

Formaldehyde, a key ingredient in embalming fluid, poses significant health and environmental risks. Traditionally, embalming fluid is injected into the body's vascular system, where it temporarily halts decomposition. The International Agency for Research on Cancer (IARC) has classified it as a possible human carcinogen, and its toxicity goes beyond the funeral home. During burial, formaldehyde leaks into the earth, contaminating groundwater and harming ecosystems.

As embalmed bodies disintegrate, toxic chemicals seep into the soil, potentially impacting nearby plant and animal life. Furthermore, formaldehyde exposure endangers the health of funeral personnel and others in the surrounding areas. The widespread use of embalming chemicals underscores the urgent need for environmentally sustainable alternatives in end-of-life practices.

Formaldehyde Usage and Disposal

The disposal of embalming fluid presents additional challenges. Funeral houses frequently flush extra embalming fluid down drains, where it enters wastewater treatment systems. While these facilities can remove certain toxins, formaldehyde remains in the environment, posing a threat to aquatic life and humans.

In light of the environmental and ethical ramifications of embalming, we are forced to reconsider traditional burial methods. The pervasive use of formaldehyde emphasizes the need for environmentally conscious alternatives that prioritize sustainability and ecological stewardship. Through discussion and raising awareness, we can move toward a more environmentally responsible approach to end-of-life care, leaving a legacy of respect and regard for both the deceased and the planet.

Disposal of Body Fluids

The disposal of body fluids (such as blood) during the burial process is a crucial aspect often overlooked. When blood is flushed down the drain in traditional burial customs, it enters the wastewater treatment system, raising serious environmental and public health concerns.

Impact on Wastewater Treatment

Blood, being a bodily fluid, carries potential pathogens and contaminants that can strain the capacity of wastewater treatment facilities. These facilities are designed to manage both organic and inorganic waste, but the addition of biological material (such as blood) might disrupt the treatment process. Blood includes organic materials that raise the biological oxygen demand (BOD) in water bodies, potentially causing oxygen depletion and damaging aquatic life (EPA, 2012).

Public Health Implications

Improper disposal of blood in burial practices can contribute to serious health issues for the general public. Blood pathogens, such as bacteria and viruses, can survive wastewater treatment processes and contaminate downstream water supplies. This pollution can cause the spread of waterborne pathogens, jeopardizing both human health and ecosystem integrity. Additionally, the presence of blood in wastewater can compromise the effectiveness of treatment methods, potentially allowing pathogens to enter the environment and affect communities located downstream.

Mitigation Measures

To address these concerns, alternative approaches to handling body fluids are being explored. Some environmentally conscious burial procedures use eco-friendly embalming chemicals or natural decomposition processes to reduce the release of toxic elements into the environment. Furthermore, advances in wastewater treatment technology (such as enhanced filtration and disinfection procedures) can help to reduce the dangers associated with disposing of blood and other human fluids.

By considering the environmental and public health implications of blood disposal in burial practices, individuals can make more informed decisions regarding end-of-life planning. Through sustainable burial practices and responsible waste management, we can minimize the impact on our environment and safeguard public health for future generations.

Reflecting on Burial Practices

As we conclude our examination of burial traditions, it is crucial to pause and contemplate the broader ramifications of our decisions. We've investigated the environmental and ethical implications of traditional burial procedures. It is evident that our burial practices, from the use of embalming chemicals to the disposal of bodily fluids, have grave consequences for both the planet and future generations.

In light of the environmental and ethical concerns surrounding traditional burial, there is a need for informed decision-making. While burial is a deeply embedded custom for many, it is vital to know that other options exist. By considering eco-friendly options such as natural burial or green cemeteries, individuals can lessen their environmental impact and maintain their values even after death (Turner, 2022).

Ultimately, let's embrace the idea that there's no one-size-fits-all approach to burial. As we navigate end-of-life decisions, we have the opportunity to choose approaches that are consistent with our values and beliefs. Whether it's opting for a biodegradable casket or forgoing embalming altogether, each decision helps to create a more sustainable and ethical approach to burial.

By researching alternative methods and taking into account their environmental impact, we can leave a legacy that honors both our lives and the planet we call home. Meanwhile, in the next chapter, we'll delve into the process and considerations surrounding cremation, shedding light on another favorable approach when it comes to honoring our loved ones while also protecting the environment.

Chapter 3:

Cremation

We now embark on an exciting adventure through the transformative process of cremation, where the earthly vessel transcends into ethereal ashes. In this chapter, we will look at cremation from a variety of perspectives, from its practical advantages to its profound cultural and environmental significance. Get ready to delve into the mechanics of cremation, understand its growing popularity, navigate the regulations and practicalities involved, and discover meaningful ways to commemorate the legacy of your deceased friends and family members while being environmentally friendly.

Understanding Cremation: A Journey Into Transformation

Enter the realm of cremation, where the solemnity of the process blends with the profound symbolism of transformation and remembrance. Cremation stands as a poignant ritual, where the physical form of the deceased travels from corporeal existence to ethereal essence, leaving behind beautiful ashes as a tribute to life's transient beauty.

Defining Cremation: From Body to Ashes

Cremation is a method in which the deceased is subjected to intense heat, typically within a specialized cremation chamber, ultimately reducing the body to ashes. This procedure typically takes around two hours, during which the organic matter is totally consumed by heat, leaving behind just bone fragments.

While the process may seem harsh, it's important to recognize the respect with which cremation is performed. Crematoriums follow specific rules to guarantee that the operation is carried out with care and expertise. Each cremation chamber is designed to hold only one deceased person at a time, ensuring a personal and dignified process.

Furthermore, cremation is a transformative process rather than a disposal strategy. The ashes produced after cremation are symbolic representations of the deceased's existence rather than tangible remains. These ashes, which often resemble fine sand, have special significance for loved ones since they serve as a tactile connection to the deceased.

In essence, cremation represents the transition from life to memory, from the tangible to the intangible. Understanding the cremation process offers light on its significance as a means of honoring and remembering the deceased, as well as offering peace and closure to those left behind.

The Mechanics of Cremation

Within the crematorium, specialized equipment stands ready to undertake the solemn task ahead (Engage Team, 2016). The heart of the operation lies in the cremation chamber, a specially designed furnace built to withstand extreme temperatures. The process begins when the deceased is gently placed inside the chamber.

Intense heat engulfs the chamber, reaching temperatures of almost 1800 degrees Fahrenheit and causing the transformation of the body into ashes. Contrary to common belief, the body is not set on fire; rather, the heat generated by the flames promotes the disintegration of organic materials, resulting in bone fragments.

The process of cremation normally takes between a half hour to two hours, depending largely on the size of the body. Throughout this time, strict protocols ensure that each individual is cremated with dignity and respect.

As the flames subside and the chamber cools, what remains is a pile of ashes, which represent the essence of the dead. Once carefully collected, these ashes become a physical token of remembrance for friends and family members to cherish.

Aside from the technical requirements, the crematorium serves as a place of meditation and farewell for those left behind. It provides a haven where the reality of loss is addressed and the mourning process begins.

In understanding the mechanics of cremation, we gain insight into a process that treats the deceased with dignity and respect, offering a profound pathway for remembrance and closure amid loss.

Cultural and Religious Perspectives on Cremation

Cremation as a practice is heavily impacted by cultural and religious beliefs, which shape how individuals and communities view the transition from life to death. Across various cultures and faiths, cremation holds diverse meanings and significance.

In Hinduism, for example, cremation is considered a sacred rite essential for the soul's journey towards liberation, or "moksha" (Weber, n.d.). The burning of the body represents the soul's release from its earthly vessel, allowing it to transcend into the afterlife. Similarly, in Buddhism, cremation is a common practice, reflecting the impermanence of life and the transitory nature of existence. Cremation is thought to aid in the soul's path toward reincarnation.

Islamic traditions, choose burial over cremation. This preference stems from religious beliefs that highlight the sacredness of the human body and the significance of keeping it intact until the Day of Resurrection.

In Christianity, the views on cremation have changed over time. While historically there was a preference for burial, many Christian denominations now recognize cremation as a valid option. The focus remains on honoring the deceased and bringing consolation to the bereaved, regardless of the chosen method of disposition. Some Christians view cremation as a practical option, while others emphasize the importance of treating the body with respect, as it is considered a temple of the Holy Spirit.

In Judaism, cremation is generally discouraged due to the belief in physical resurrection. Traditional Jewish burial rituals include interring the deceased in the ground, emphasizing the body's holiness and eventual return to the earth. However, if cremation is deemed necessary (such as during an epidemic or in dire circumstances), some Jewish communities may allow it under specified conditions and rites.

Aside from these major religions, cremation is associated with a wide range of cultural traditions and beliefs. In Japan, for instance, cremation has been the predominant method of disposition for centuries due to limited burial space. Japanese cremation rituals often involve complex ceremonies that express a strong reverence for the deceased and their passage into the afterlife.

Overall, cultural and religious opinions on cremation differ greatly, but they all have one thing in common: They recognize death as a transformational process and emphasize the need to honor the deceased with dignity and reverence.

Factors Influencing the Rise of Cremation

Cost-Effectiveness and Financial Flexibility

Unlike traditional burials, which often involve costly elements such as caskets, burial plots, and headstones, cremation tends to be more budget-friendly. The absence of these expenses can alleviate financial burdens, allowing families to reallocate funds toward other aspects of honoring the memory of the departed. Cremation allows families to express their love and respect in a variety of ways, including organizing a meaningful memorial ceremony, producing personalized keepsakes, and contributing to charity causes in the deceased's name.

Moreover, cremation offers financial predictability, as the costs associated with cremation services are generally more transparent and straightforward compared to traditional burial expenses. With fewer factors to consider, families can better plan and manage their budgets, thus lessening the stress that comes with financial uncertainty during times of loss.

Beyond the immediate financial considerations, many families are concerned about the long-term maintenance costs involved with traditional burial locations. Cremation reduces the need for ongoing cemetery upkeep fees, offering peace of mind knowing that there are no additional financial obligations down the line.

Addressing Space Constraints and Eco-Consciousness

As cities grow and available land for burials becomes limited, the environmental consequences of traditional burial practices become more apparent. Cemeteries, which often expand and occupy large areas of land, contribute to urban sprawl and encroach on natural habitats. Furthermore, maintaining these burial locations takes resources such as water and energy, which puts additional strain on environmental sustainability efforts.

In contrast, cremation presents a more eco-friendly alternative. By reducing the deceased's remains to ashes, cremation eliminates the need for burial grounds, thereby conserving valuable land space. This is particularly significant in densely populated areas where land is scarce. The compact nature of cremation facilities also means they require less physical space than cemeteries, making them a more practical alternative in urban areas.

Furthermore, cremation can have a lower carbon footprint compared to traditional burials. While cremation emits carbon dioxide and other gases into the atmosphere, it produces fewer greenhouse gases than embalming and maintaining burial grounds. In addition, advances in cremation technology have resulted in more energy-efficient crematoriums, further lowering the environmental impact.

For individuals who prioritize environmental sustainability, choosing cremation aligns with their values of reducing their ecological footprint. By opting for cremation, they can feel confident that their final journey will be less harmful to the planet. This decision reflects a growing awareness of the environmental repercussions of end-of-life practices and a commitment to making choices that safeguard the well-being of future generations.

Streamlining End-of-Life Arrangements

Families who choose cremation often find comfort in the process's simplicity. Unlike traditional burials, which involve multiple logistical arrangements such as selecting a burial plot and casket and coordinating with cemetery staff, cremation streamlines these aspects. With cremation, there's no need to worry about the complexities of embalming or the long-term maintenance of a gravesite. Instead, families can concentrate on honoring their loved one's memory without the extra stress of lengthy planning and coordination.

Additionally, cremation offers families greater flexibility in memorialization options. Whether dispersing ashes in a place of importance, interring them in a columbarium, or keeping them in an urn at home, cremation allows people to personalize the final resting place of their dear ones in a way that resonates with their individual preferences and beliefs. This flexibility enables the creation of personalized and meaningful tributes, such as custom urns, artwork, and even jewelry, that honor the unique life and legacy of their departed friends or family members.

Navigating the Cremation Process: Regulations and Practicalities

Waiting Periods and Organ Donation Procedures

Understanding waiting periods and organ donation protocols is essential when navigating the legal landscape around cremation. Consider the following:

- For starters, there is usually a mandated waiting period after an individual's death before cremation can take place. This waiting period varies by jurisdiction and is usually imposed to guarantee adequate documentation and to accommodate any legal procedures, such as the issuance of death certificates. The duration of this waiting period varies depending on local rules; however, it is often between 24 and 48 hours.

- Additionally, if the deceased is an organ donor, specific procedures must be followed before cremation can take place (Powell, 2023). Organ donation is a wonderful act of kindness that can save lives, but it necessitates close collaboration among medical professionals, the deceased's family, and the appropriate authorities. Organs must be removed as soon as possible after death to remain viable for transplantation. This process is conducted in a respectful and dignified manner, honoring the wishes of the donor and their family.

- Furthermore, it's essential to understand that bodily fluids and organs do not need to be removed before cremation. Contrary to common misconceptions, the cremation procedure is intended to manage all of the deceased's remains, including bodily fluids and organs. However, if the deceased was an organ donor, the necessary organ retrieval procedures are carried out separately, usually in a hospital environment, before the body is sent to the crematorium.

Removal of Items Before Cremation Procedures

Before the cremation process commences, there's an important step that involves the removal of certain items from the deceased (Kaplan, n.d.). This procedure ensures the safety of both the individual and the cremation equipment while following legislation and practical considerations.

Typically, things that could disrupt the cremation process or endanger the crematorium staff are carefully removed. This includes objects such as jewelry, pacemakers, prosthetics, and clothing. Jewelry and other metallic items, for instance, can damage the cremation equipment or cause potential hazards during the process. Pacemakers, on the other hand, contain batteries that can explode when subjected to high temperatures, posing a serious threat to cremation workers' safety.

Additionally, removing personal effects ensures that they do not become damaged or lost during the cremation process, thus allowing family and friends to keep them as heirlooms. Clothing is usually removed to facilitate the efficient and thorough cremation of the body. Synthetic materials like rubber, vinyl, and latex, commonly found in shoes and clothing, can release toxic chemicals when burned, posing environmental and health risks. As a result, to ensure a clean and eco-friendly process, people are often cremated without shoes or synthetic clothing.

Understanding these procedures not only demystifies the cremation process but also emphasizes the importance of safety, respect, and adherence to regulations. By ensuring that potentially hazardous items are removed beforehand, crematorium staff can perform their duties efficiently and safely, while families can have peace of mind knowing that their deceased are being treated with the utmost care and decency during this final farewell.

Debunking Myths

There are numerous misconceptions about the cremation procedure, ranging from the dread of flames engulfing the body to concerns about genetic privacy and environmental damage. These instances of misunderstanding often lead to individuals making incorrect assumptions about the procedure's nature and outcomes.

- One common myth suggests that cremation involves setting the body on fire. In actuality, the technique uses extreme heat, which reaches soaring temperatures, to convert the body into ashes. This controlled environment ensures a dignified transition without flames destroying the body.

- Another misconception concerns the removal of body organs before cremation. Contrary to popular belief, there's no need to remove organs or bodily fluids before the cremation process. The body is respectfully placed in the cremation chamber as is, with no alterations needed.

- Some individuals worry about the possibility of obtaining DNA from ashes, believing it may compromise privacy or lead to unforeseen consequences. However, DNA cannot be retrieved from the actual ashes due to the high temperatures involved in the cremation process (Day, 2022). This reassures families who are concerned about genetic privacy.

- Furthermore, there's a prevailing notion that cremation is harmful to the environment (Mendoza, 2023). While cremation can generate carbon dioxide and other gases, current crematoriums use advanced filtration systems to reduce environmental impact. Additionally, some facilities offer eco-friendly alternatives such as renewable energy sources or carbon offset programs.

- Finally, there is a common misconception that cremation is a short process that takes only minutes. In reality, the length of cremation varies depending on body size and composition. Completing the process professionally and respectfully can take anywhere from less than an hour to more.

By dispelling these myths and acquiring accurate information, we can make informed decisions regarding end-of-life planning, thus ensuring a meaningful and dignified farewell for the beloved person we have lost.

As we conclude our exploration of cremation (which, as we have established, is a deeply personal and transformative process), we now turn our focus to another approach of leaving a lasting impact: whole body donation to science. In this next chapter, we learn about the profound opportunity to contribute to medical research and education, thus getting a glimpse into the noble act of advancing knowledge and healing even beyond life's earthly confines. Read on as we embark on an adventure of understanding the invaluable legacy left by the selfless donation of one's body to science.

Chapter 4:

Whole Body Donation to

Science

In the world of medical science, there's a remarkable act of generosity: donating one's body to advance knowledge. This chapter explores the process of whole-body donation, from initial considerations to its huge impact on medical education. It's a story of selflessness and the enduring legacy of those who choose to contribute to scientific progress even after their time has passed.

Understanding the Gift

Whole-body donation is a profoundly generous act that holds the power to shape the future of medicine and healthcare. It is a selfless decision made during one's life to help enhance medical education, training, and scientific research after death. But what exactly constitutes complete body donation, and why is it so important?

Allow me to share a personal anecdote to illustrate the significance of this choice. One of my sisters is a nurse practitioner, deeply passionate about unraveling the mysteries of the human body. Her quest for knowledge has always been evident in her career. While she hasn't explicitly discussed her end-of-life plans with me, I can envision body donation as something she might consider. Her commitment to advancing medical knowledge, even beyond her lifetime, is consistent with the spirit of whole-body donation.

One of the key aspects of whole-body donation is informed consent. This means that donors decide to donate their bodies for medical reasons while they are still alive. This consent is often given through advance directives, which are legal documents defining a person's healthcare choices; or donor registry systems, in which people formally register their intention to donate their bodies after death. By providing informed consent, donors ensure that their wishes are respected and that their bodies are used in accordance with their desires.

Once a person has decided to donate their body, it becomes a valuable resource for medical education, training, and research. Medical students, aspiring surgeons, and other healthcare professionals use donated bodies to learn human anatomy in a hands-on environment (Booth, 2018). In addition to education and training, donated bodies serve an important part in scientific studies. Anatomical specimens are used by researchers to investigate a variety of medical ailments, diseases, and treatment possibilities. Scientists obtain essential insights into the inner workings of the human body by dissecting and scrutinizing donated bodies, thus resulting in advances in medical science and improved patient care.

Ultimately, whole-body donation is not only a selfless act but also a deeply impactful one. It helps equip future generations of healthcare professionals with the information and skills necessary to save lives and alleviate suffering. It contributes to groundbreaking research with the potential to transform healthcare and enhance patient outcomes around the world. Perhaps most importantly, it commemorates the legacy of donors who, even after death, continue to make a significant difference in the lives of others.

Importance in Medical Education and Research

Assume you're a medical student, eager to learn and comprehend the complexities of the human body. You've spent hours studying textbooks, memorizing anatomical pictures, and listening to lectures. But something is missing: a hands-on experience that actually brings the topic to life. Here's where whole-body donation comes in.

When people selflessly donate their bodies to medical organizations, they give future doctors, surgeons, and healthcare workers an incredible opportunity. Students can work with actual human cadavers rather than just textbooks or computer models. This hands-on experience is unparalleled in its educational value.

Picture yourself in an anatomy lab, surrounded by classmates and a donated cadaver lying in front of you. You gently dissect the body, examining the intricate network of muscles, nerves, and organs. As you investigate, you get a deeper grasp of human anatomy that lectures and illustrations cannot provide.

Through the use of donated cadavers, students can gain invaluable experience in surgical methods within a safe and regulated environment. They learn how to suture wounds, identify vital structures, and perform procedures with precision. This practical experience is essential for developing the skills and confidence needed to excel in their future careers.

But whole body donation isn't just about learning anatomy or honing surgical skills. It also involves instilling empathy and compassion in future healthcare practitioners. As students work with donated cadavers, they gain a great appreciation for those who have generously contributed to their education. They learn to treat each patient with dignity and compassion, acknowledging the humanity in everyone they serve.

In addition to training future doctors and surgeons, whole-body donation also supports other healthcare disciplines. Physical therapists, occupational therapists, and medical researchers all benefit from access to anatomical specimens. These professionals use donated cadavers to study disease processes, test new treatments, and develop innovative medical equipment.

How Does the Process Work?

Making the decision to donate your body after death is an important step, one that reflects your personal perspectives (Brouillette, 2022). For many, the decision is rooted in a deep-seated desire to contribute to the advancement of medical science and education. It's about leaving a lasting legacy, a gift that continues to benefit others even after you're gone.

But this decision isn't made lightly. It's a process that involves introspection, reflection, and conversations with loved ones. You might find yourself pondering questions like: What do I want my legacy to be? How can I have a meaningful impact even after I die? These are weighty questions, but ones that ultimately lead to a decision based on selflessness and compassion.

Your decision to donate your body is guided by your values and beliefs. Perhaps you believe in the value of education and the power of knowledge to transform lives. Or maybe you've experienced firsthand the impact of medical research and want to contribute to its continual progress. Whatever your motivation, know that your decision holds the potential to make a real difference in the lives of others.

Nevertheless, it's crucial to take the time to carefully consider your decision and ensure that it aligns with your wishes and values. This could include looking into different donation programs, learning about the donation procedure, and comprehending the potential benefits and ramifications of donation. It is also crucial to share your decision with your loved ones, ensuring that they understand your choice.

Exploring Personal Values and Ethical Considerations

When contemplating the decision to donate one's body to medical science, it's essential to embark on a journey of introspection, considering personal values and ethical principles (Sieger, 2018).

Reflecting on Personal Beliefs

At the core of the decision to donate one's body lies a consideration of deeply held personal beliefs. For many, this decision provides an opportunity to leave a lasting impact on society, contributing to the greater good even beyond death. Taking the time to focus on one's principles can help explain reasons and give one a sense of purpose while making decisions.

Some may find that their values align closely with the principles of altruism and compassion, viewing body donation as a selfless act aimed at benefiting future generations. Others may be inspired by a desire to promote scientific growth and innovation, viewing the donation as a chance to contribute to medical breakthroughs that might ease human suffering.

Ethical Reflection

The ethical implications of body donation involve a range of factors, including autonomy, dignity, and the broader societal impact of medical research (Balta et al., 2022). Autonomy refers to the right of individuals to make decisions about their bodies, including the choice to donate organs or tissues for transplantation or medical education.

Maintaining dignity throughout the donation process is paramount, ensuring that the individual's wishes are respected and that their body is treated with the utmost respect and reverence. It is important to bear in mind that, while the body may be exploited for scientific research, it is nevertheless entitled to dignity and ethical treatment.

Moreover, contemplating the greater good of medical research and education can provide a broader perspective on the ethical implications of body donation. Donors help to improve healthcare outcomes and address important medical concerns by contributing to the advancement of knowledge and the training of future healthcare professionals.

Seeking Guidance

For some individuals, the decision to donate their body to medical science may raise complex moral and spiritual questions. In such instances, consulting with spiritual or ethical counselors can provide useful insight and assistance. These advisers can provide a forum for contemplation and discussion, assisting individuals in navigating the ethical considerations around body donation.

Seeking advice from clergy members, ethicists, or other trusted mentors can help people attain clarity and peace of mind in their decision-making process. Furthermore, meeting with healthcare professionals or representatives from medical institutions can provide useful information while also addressing any issues or questions that may emerge.

Conversations about end-of-life decisions can be difficult, but they are necessary for ensuring that your wishes are understood and respected. By honestly addressing your decision with your loved ones, you can provide them peace of mind and clarity during a challenging period. Together, you can navigate the process of whole-body donation with understanding and support.

Discussing Intentions With Loved Ones

Open and honest communication with loved ones about your intentions for body disposition is necessary (MedCure, 2019). While it may seem like a difficult conversation to have, it can ultimately provide reassurance for both you and your family. Here's why it's important to have this discussion:

Importance of Open Dialogue

Talking openly about your wishes regarding body donation helps your loved ones understand and respect your choices. It ensures that your desires are understood and can be fulfilled when the time comes. By starting this conversation, you are taking proactive steps to avoid any potential confusion or dispute among family members.

Addressing Concerns

Your decision to donate your body to medical research may cause questions or concerns among your family and friends. Some may be concerned about the emotional or practical ramifications of the donating process. By providing an opportunity for them to express these concerns, you create a supportive environment where everyone's feelings are acknowledged and addressed.

Facilitating Understanding

Explaining why you choose to donate your body can assist your loved ones in comprehending your point of view. Sharing your objectives, whether they are a desire to contribute to medical research, a devotion to education, or simply a personal belief, encourages empathy and support from those who are close to you. By sharing your reasoning, you invite your loved ones to see the value and significance of your choice.

Initiating the Conversation

Addressing the topic of body donation may feel daunting, but it's essential to approach it with sensitivity and openness. Choose a time when everyone is calm and relaxed and there are no distractions. You might begin the conversation by expressing your desire to discuss your end-of-life wishes and assuring your loved ones that it is acceptable to discuss sensitive topics.

Sharing Your Intentions

When addressing your desire to give your body, be straightforward about your intentions. Explain what body donation means and why you are drawn to this option. Share any study you've done on the subject, and clear up any misconceptions or anxieties your loved ones may have. Reassure them that your decision is thoughtfully considered and aligns with your values and beliefs.

Listening to Their Thoughts

Encourage your loved ones to share their thoughts and feelings about your decision. Let them know that their feedback is valuable and that you are eager to resolve any concerns they may have. Be patient and empathetic as they process the information and offer support and reassurance as needed.

Creating a Plan Together

Once you've discussed your intentions, consider developing a plan together as a family. This may include documenting your wishes in writing, designating a spokesperson to communicate with medical professionals, or exploring options for memorial services. By involving your loved ones in the planning phase, you can guarantee that everyone is on the same page and that your wishes are followed when the time comes.

Resources and Support for Those Considering Body Donation

Accessing Information

When considering body donation, access to accurate and complete information is crucial. Fortunately, there are numerous resources available to help you make this decision with clarity and confidence (PCRM, n.d.).

- **Pamphlets:** Many medical institutions and organizations provide informational pamphlets that outline the process of body donation in detail. These pamphlets usually address issues such as eligibility requirements, donation procedures, and commonly asked questions. They are useful reference materials that you can peruse at your leisure to get a better idea of what to expect.

- **Websites:** In today's digital age, the internet provides a wealth of information on practically any subject, and body donation is no exception. Numerous reliable websites provide detailed information regarding body donation, such as step-by-step tutorials, FAQs, and contact information for relevant organizations. These websites often include information about the advantages of body donation, testimonials from donors and their families, and the influence of donated bodies on medical education and research.

- **Helplines:** If you have specific questions or concerns about body donation that you'd like to have answered in real time, helplines can be quite useful. Many organizations that promote body donation have helplines staffed by trained professionals who can provide specialized advice. Whether you're unclear about the eligibility requirements, need clarification on the donation process, or simply need someone to talk to about your decision, helplines offer support and guidance every step of the way.

Support Networks

Deciding to donate your body to research can be an extremely personal and sometimes difficult matter.

Having a support network to draw on can make a significant difference in navigating this path.

- **Support groups:** Joining a support group for individuals considering body donation (or those who have already made the decision) can provide invaluable emotional support and practical advice. These groups often consist of people who have had similar experiences and can provide empathy, encouragement, and solidarity. Whether in-person or online, support groups create a safe space for open discussion, sharing of concerns, and celebration of the decision to contribute to medical science.

- **Organizations:** There are various organizations dedicated to assisting people with the body donation process. These groups may provide a variety of services, such as educational resources, counseling, and aid with logistics. Connecting with such groups allows you to gain access to a plethora of information and experience, which can help you make a more confident and educated decision.

- **Family and friends:** Finally, do not underestimate the importance of family and friends' support. Discussing your aims with family and close friends can help you feel validated and enhance your resolve. While they may have their own questions or concerns, involving them in the decision-making process can promote understanding and support for your choice.

Professional Guidance

While information and support networks can be useful, you may occasionally want more specific help from healthcare professionals or medical institution representatives (Research for Life, n.d.).

- **Consultation:** Consider meeting with a healthcare expert, such as your primary care physician or an end-of-life specialist. These professionals can offer medical insights, address any health-related concerns you may have, and provide assistance suited to your specific needs.

- **Medical institution representatives:** If you are thinking about giving your body to a certain medical facility, contacting their representatives can be helpful. These experts may provide in-depth information regarding the institution's body donation program, including eligibility requirements, donation procedures, and any associated charges. They may also answer any specific questions or concerns you may have, ensuring that you feel fully informed and comfortable with your decision.

Post-Donation Arrangements

After making the honorable decision to donate one's body to science, both the donor and their loved ones should be aware of the necessary post-donation procedures. These arrangements ensure that the donation process runs smoothly and that the donor's preferences are met respectfully.

Transporting the Body to the Facility

Once a person has passed away and their decision to donate their body has been communicated to the appropriate authorities or medical institutions, the next step is arranging for the transportation of the body to the designated facility. Typically, the medical facility or organization accepting the donation coordinates this transportation. Families of the deceased may be required to submit specific information, such as the location of the body and any relevant paperwork, to facilitate the transportation process.

It's important to note that the cost of transporting the body to the facility may vary depending on location and distance. Some medical organizations cover transportation costs as part of their donation program, while others may ask the donor's family to bear the cost. Therefore, donors and their families should inquire about transportation arrangements and associated costs in advance.

Understanding the Facility's Policies

Each medical institution or anatomical donation program has its own set of policies and procedures for accepting and using donated bodies (Anatomical Sciences, n.d.). Donors and their families need to familiarize themselves with these policies to ensure that their wishes are respected and that they understand how their bodies will be utilized for educational or research purposes.

These policies may include guidelines on the types of donations accepted, eligibility criteria for donors, consent procedures, and the handling of donated remains. Furthermore, some organizations may have special standards for the donor's medical history, cause of death, or certain disqualifying factors. By understanding the facility's policies, donors can make informed decisions about their donation and ensure that their wishes align with the institution's procedures.

Ensuring Eventual Disposition of Remains

While the primary purpose of whole-body donation is to contribute to medical education and research, donors and their families should also consider the eventual disposition of the remains. Medical institutions normally handle the disposition of donated bodies with care and dignity, ensuring that the remains are treated in accordance with the donor's wishes and any applicable legal requirements.

Depending on the institution's policies and the donor's wishes, the remains may be cremated or buried following the culmination of their educational or research objectives (NJSFDA, n.d.). Some institutions offer options for the return of cremated remains to the donor's family, while others may have communal burial or scattering arrangements. Donors need to have a discussion with their relatives and the accepting institution regarding their preferences for the disposition of their remains to guarantee that their wishes are honored.

Ultimately, in a world where medical knowledge is continually evolving, whole-body donation represents hope and development. It reminds us that, even in our final moments, we can leave behind a legacy of kindness, generosity, and healing. So, as you consider your end-of-life plans, think about the profound impact you could have through this type of disposition because, in giving the gift of yourself, you're giving the gift of life.

As we conclude our discussion on body donation, we transition to exploring another alternative to traditional burial: green or natural burial. This eco-friendly approach aligns with the ideals of sustainability and environmental protection, offering a harmonious way to return to the earth. Prepare to explore the beauty and significance of green burial practices, which honor the interdependence of life and nature.

Chapter 5:

Green (or Natural) Burial

A few years ago, my friend Anne told me a truly moving story that forever changed my perspective on end-of-life traditions. It revolved around her loving grandma Kathy, who had always had a strong connection to nature. Anne characterized Kathy as a soul that found refuge and tranquility in the embrace of nature, her spirit intertwined with the whispering leaves and the song of birds. As Kathy's life journey came to a close, she expressed a strong wish to return to the land in a way that reflected her deep love for nature.

In the final days of her life, Kathy expressed her final wish: a green burial. It is a concept not unfamiliar to many in our circle, but as Anne recounted the story, the beauty and significance of Kathy's choice became abundantly clear. Anne described how, together with their family, they embarked on a poignant journey to fulfill Kathy's wish. They looked for a peaceful natural burial area, a sacred sanctuary where the earthly and spiritual realms converged seamlessly.

The landscape they encountered was nothing short of breathtaking. It was a peaceful expanse of woodland terrain with wildflowers dancing in the breeze and sunlight filtering through the lush canopy above. It was a place where the boundaries between life and death appeared to blur, where every rustle of leaves spoke stories of eternity and every ray of sunlight witnessed the cycle of regeneration.

On the day of Kathy's burial, friends and family gathered under the open sky, surrounded by nature's soothing embrace. There were tears, of course, at the loss of a beloved matriarch, but there was also a profound sense of peace, knowing that Kathy's final resting place would nurture new life, serving as a living tribute to her unwavering love for the natural world.

As Anne told this moving story, I was struck by the concept of green burial—an alternate method of burying our loved ones that resonates deeply with our innate connection to the earth. It's more than just a method of burial; it's a profound understanding of our interconnectedness with the natural world. It's a realization that, even after death, we remain a part of life's rich tapestry.

The significance of green burial extends far beyond its environmental implications. At its core, it's a deeply spiritual practice, a way of returning to the earth with reverence and gratitude, acknowledging the cycle of life and death that nurtures us all. By selecting a green burial, we demonstrate our resolve to tread softly on the land, leaving behind a legacy of stewardship and respect for future generations.

In the pages that follow, we'll look deeper into the concept of green burial, including its principles, practices, and cultural importance. We'll investigate the secrets of decomposition, look at the practical ramifications, and think about the bigger picture for our planet and our collective consciousness. Above all, we'll endeavor to understand the tremendous knowledge contained within this ancient yet ageless ritual, a wisdom that speaks to the very essence of what it means to be human, to love, and, finally, to return to the ground on which we lived.

Understanding Green Burial

Green burial stands as a beacon of environmental consciousness amid the traditions of conventional burial practices. It's a deviation from the norm, a conscious decision to prioritize sustainability and accept the natural cycle of life and death.

In contrast to traditional burials, which include embalming bodies with chemicals and encasing them in concrete vaults, green burial takes a different approach. It eliminates the layers of artificiality, favoring simplicity and a strong respect for the environment.

Picture this: Rather than a locked casket contained in a sterile chamber, a body is laid to rest directly in the ground, where wildflowers sway gently in the breeze and sunshine pours through the canopy of trees. It's a gift to the ground in its purest form, allowing the body to decay properly and return to the soil.

By forgoing embalming chemicals and concrete vaults, green burial minimizes its environmental impact. It's a conscious choice to tread lightly on the planet, leaving a legacy of stewardship rather than pollution. In a society struggling with the repercussions of climate change and environmental degradation, green burial provides a ray of hope, a means to honor the earth even after death.

Consider the positive impact of green burials, which contribute to the formation of fertile soil rather than filling landfills with nonbiodegradable waste. They join the cycle of renewal, nourishing the soil and sustaining future generations of life.

A Natural Return to the Earth

Green burial represents a return to the timeless rhythms of nature (Elliott, 2019). Instead of preserving the body in a state of artificial stasis, it allows us to succumb to the unstoppable forces of decay and renewal. In doing so, we become part of a larger cycle, one that extends beyond individual existence and ties us to the larger web of life.

This incorporation into the natural cycle serves both symbolic and practical purposes. By returning our remains to the planet in a sustainable manner, we ensure that our legacy is one of sustenance, not depletion. Our bodies feed the soil, supplying essential nutrients for both plants and bacteria. In this way, we contribute to the continued vitality of the ecosystem, sustaining a legacy of regeneration and abundance.

The Depth of Burial and Its Implications

In green burial, where the body is laid to rest isn't just a matter of tradition; it's a vital part of the process that ensures minimal environmental impact and maximum ecological benefit. Green burials are often conducted at a depth of 3.5 to 4 feet below the Earth's surface (Green Burial Council, n.d.). This depth is not picked at random; it has been deliberately selected to promote optimal decomposition while protecting the surrounding environment.

At this level, several crucial elements come into play. The first and most important consideration is oxygenation. By burying the body at this depth, oxygen levels are maintained, allowing for aerobic decay. This means that bacteria responsible for breaking down organic matter can thrive and decompose the body in an environmentally healthy way. Essentially, the soil becomes a bustling ecosystem of tiny organisms working to return the body to its natural elements.

Another important consideration is protection against scavengers. Burying the body farther underground makes it less accessible to animals looking for food. This preserves the dignity of the departed while also preventing disturbances at the burial place.

Furthermore, burial at this level serves as a barrier to the leaching of decompositional byproducts into groundwater. This is essential for maintaining water quality and ensuring that surrounding ecosystems remain healthy and vibrant.

By adhering to these burial practices, green burials contribute to the maintenance of ecological balance. Rather than interrupting natural processes or introducing hazardous elements into the environment, green burials promote sustainability and respect for the Earth's fragile ecosystems.

Environmental Benefits and Growing Popularity

Green burial, as a sustainable end-of-life option, provides a host of environmental benefits that resonate deeply with individuals looking for eco-conscious alternatives (Stuart-Ulin, 2019). By embracing green burial practices, individuals contribute to the preservation of our planet in several meaningful ways.

First and foremost, green burial does not employ embalming chemicals or nonbiodegradable materials, which are often associated with traditional burial procedures. Embalming fluids, which often contain formaldehyde and other harmful compounds, can contaminate the soil and groundwater, endangering ecosystems and public health. By eschewing these chemicals, green burial reduces pollution and minimizes the environmental footprint of the final resting place.

Moreover, the absence of concrete vaults or elaborate caskets enables green burial sites to return to their natural state more rapidly. Without the hindrance of nonbiodegradable materials, these areas become more suitable for the restoration of biodiversity and the preservation of natural habitats. Over time, green burial grounds can evolve into dynamic ecosystems, providing sanctuaries for native flora and fauna.

As awareness of environmental issues continues to grow, so too does the popularity of green burial. More and more individuals are turning to this sustainable option to align their values with their final resting place.

Furthermore, the growing availability of green burial options in the United States and around the world makes it more accessible to those who wish to leave a lighter footprint on the environment in their final moments. Whether motivated by a deep connection to nature or a desire to reduce their ecological impact, people are adopting green burial as a meaningful and responsible choice for their end-of-life arrangements.

Key Features of Green Burial

Decomposition Process: Natural Decay Without Embalming

In a green burial, the focus is on letting nature take its course. Instead of interrupting the body's natural journey back to the earth with embalming chemicals, green burial allows for a gentle return to the soil. Traditionally, embalming fluids are used to preserve the body for viewing, but green burial eliminates this step. These chemicals, while intended to prevent decomposition, can be hazardous to the environment. Green burial honors nature's delicate balance by allowing it to decompose naturally.

As time passes, the body gradually decomposes, returning to the earth from where it originated. This procedure is aided by using biodegradable materials for the coffin or shroud. Without the barrier of embalming chemicals or materials that don't decompose, the body can easily reintegrate with the soil, nourishing the earth in the process.

This approach is not only environmentally friendly but also consistent with our basic connection to nature. It's a way of honoring our loved ones in a manner that reflects their appreciation for the beauty and cycles of the natural world. In essence, green burial is more than just saying goodbye, it's about giving back to the earth, leaving behind a legacy of sustainability and environmental stewardship.

Types of Caskets and Shrouds: Biodegradable Materials

The use of caskets or shrouds in green burial practices is crucial for achieving environmental sustainability and honoring the natural cycle of life (Barrett, 2019). Unlike traditional burial procedures, which often involve expensive, undegradable materials, green burials embrace simplicity and eco-consciousness.

- **Wicker:** Imagine a casket fashioned from natural materials such as willow or bamboo, exuding rustic charm and artisanal craftsmanship. Wicker caskets offer a beautiful, earthy appearance while being completely biodegradable. As they return to the earth, these woven wonders decompose gracefully, merging seamlessly into the surrounding soil.

- **Cardboard:** For those seeking a minimalist approach to their final resting place, cardboard caskets provide a simple yet respectable solution. Made from recycled materials, these eco-friendly containers offer a sustainable alternative to traditional hardwood caskets. Despite their simple appearance, cardboard caskets convey a powerful message of environmental sustainability.

- **Natural wood:** Envision a coffin constructed of natural wood, such as pine, with its warm colors and natural grains on full display. Unlike treated or varnished wood, these caskets are left untreated and unpolished, enabling them to degrade naturally over time. The wood gradually decomposes, nourishing the soil and enriching the earth with its organic essence.

- **Linen or cotton shrouds:** The smooth, natural fibers of a linen or cotton shroud provide consolation to the dead. These breathable textiles softly embrace the body, allowing for a dignified decay while preserving the individual's connection to nature. Wrapped in layers of fabric, the deceased embark on their journey back to the soil, leaving behind a legacy of sustainability and respect for nature.

The Innovative Option: Mushroom Burial Suit by Coeio

Coeio's mushroom burial suit is a novel concept that is altering traditional funeral practices (Ever Loved, 2023). This one-of-a-kind garment offers a revolutionary alternative to traditional burial practices, providing a holistic approach to environmentally friendly funeral ceremonies.

This burial suit is made of biodegradable materials that have been infused with mushroom spores. It represents sustainability from start to end. Unlike traditional burial garments, which usually contribute to environmental damage with nonbiodegradable components, this suit allows for a natural return to the earth.

The mushroom spores embedded in the fabric act as natural decomposers, aiding in the breakdown of the body and simultaneously filtering toxins. As the body decomposes, the mushrooms perform an important function in turning organic matter into essential nutrients for the soil, promoting soil regeneration and environmental health.

This creative approach not only represents a growing awareness of environmental sustainability but also promotes a stronger connection to nature in the final stages of life. It represents a shift away from traditional funeral rituals and toward a more harmonious relationship between humanity and the natural world.

Furthermore, the mushroom burial suit represents a significant shift in how we perceive death and its impact on the environment. It invites us to reconsider our approach to end-of-life rituals, viewing them not as separate from nature but as integral to its cyclical processes.

In essence, Coeio's mushroom burial suit is not just a garment; it's a testament to our interconnectedness with the earth. It consoles bereaved families while also making a good contribution to the environment. By embracing creative solutions like these, we open the road for a more sustainable and compassionate approach to honoring life and death.

Limitations on Memorial Markers in Green Burial Cemeteries

Green burial sites employ a unique approach to memorial markers that complement the natural landscape (Hoffner, 2018). Unlike traditional cemeteries, which have elaborate headstones and monuments dotting the landscape, green burial sites promote the preservation of nature's beauty and ecological balance.

Imagine walking into a green burial cemetery and being greeted by gently swaying native grasses and exquisite wildflowers blooming rather than rows of foreboding headstones. This is the essence of green burial: a final resting place that merges with the surrounding landscape, creating a sense of peace and connectedness with nature.

Instead of typical markers that can disrupt the natural flow of the ecosystem, green cemeteries promote alternatives that honor both the deceased and the planet. One such idea is to use native plants. These indigenous flora not only serve as living memorials but also contribute to the ecosystem by providing a habitat for local wildlife and promoting biodiversity.

Another alternative to traditional markers is engraved rocks. Smooth stones bearing personalized inscriptions can be placed at burial sites, offering a lasting remembrance that blends seamlessly with the earth. These stones, weathered by time and the elements, become part of the landscape, representing the enduring bond between loved ones and the natural world.

In addition to native plants and engraved rocks, biodegradable markers are also favored in these cemeteries. Made from sustainable materials such as recycled paper or plant-based resins, these markers gently decompose over time, leaving behind no trace of their presence. This minimalist approach to memorialization reflects the concept of environmental protection.

By embracing these limitations on memorial markers, green burial cemeteries uphold a profound reverence for nature and promote a deeper connection to the earth. Each burial site serves as not only a resting place for the deceased but also a living tribute to the natural world's beauty and resilience.

Availability and Practical Considerations

Availability of Green Burial Cemeteries Across the United States

In recent years, there has been a remarkable surge in the availability of green burial cemeteries across the United States (Funeral Basics, n.d.). What was once considered a niche or unusual option is now more widely available to individuals and families seeking environmentally friendly burial options. This trend reflects an increasing demand for burial techniques that promote environmental sustainability and naturalism.

A number of factors contribute to the growing popularity of green burial grounds. For starters, increased knowledge of environmental issues has led many people to seek out more eco-friendly end-of-life approaches. Furthermore, a desire for simplicity and a return to nature has prompted people to reevaluate traditional burial practices in favor of green alternatives.

Today, green burial cemeteries can be found in nearly every state, offering a range of options for those seeking a final resting place that reflects their values. These cemeteries often offer beautiful and natural surroundings, creating a peaceful and soothing environment for family and friends to visit and remember.

However, it's important to note that the availability of green cemeteries may vary depending on location. While certain regions have plenty of options, others may have few or none at all. Therefore, individuals interested in green burial should take the time to research and inquire about the availability of such cemeteries in their specific area.

Fortunately, as the demand for green burial options increases, more cemeteries are beginning to provide these services. Additionally, advocacy and awareness campaigns are helping to educate the public about the benefits of green burial, which is driving the expansion of these facilities.

Overall, the growing number of green burial cemeteries in the United States represents a good shift toward more sustainable and ecologically conscientious end-of-life practices. Individuals who choose green burial can leave behind a legacy of care for the world while also honoring their loved ones in a meaningful and environmentally friendly way.

Duration of Decomposition Based on Soil Type, Oxygen, and Moisture

Understanding the duration of decomposition in green burial is crucial for appreciating its ecological significance and ensuring a sustainable return to the earth. Several factors affect this process, including soil type, oxygen levels, and moisture content.

In green burial, the body's process of natural decomposition begins as soon as the body is laid to rest in the earth. However, the rate of degradation varies according to environmental conditions.

One important factor is soil type. Microbial activity varies between soils and plays an important role in the breakdown of organic matter. Well-aerated soils with an adequate oxygen supply promote rapid decomposition by encouraging microbial activity. In such soils, the bulk of soft tissue can decompose in as little as six weeks, helped by moisture absorption (Webster, n.d.).

Moisture content also affects decomposition. Adequate moisture is necessary to sustain microbial life and aid in the breakdown of organic material. In moist soils, decomposition progresses faster than in dry soils. However, excessive moisture can inhibit decomposition by creating anaerobic conditions, slowing down the process.

Oxygen availability is another critical factor. Aerobic decomposition, which occurs in the presence of oxygen, is typically faster and more efficient than anaerobic decomposition. Well-aerated soils provide aerobic conditions, allowing microorganisms to thrive and speed up decomposition.

Despite these factors, total decomposition (including bone absorption) may take up to two years or longer, particularly in moist soils. The timeline of decomposition emphasizes the importance of considering long-term ecological consequences when opting for green burial. By allowing the body to return to the earth naturally, green burial enhances soil health and fertility, contributing to the overall sustainability of the ecosystem.

Understanding the dynamics of decomposition in green burial enhances our appreciation for its environmental benefits and underscores the importance of choosing burial practices with low ecological impact.

Cultural Acceptance of Green Burial Within the Catholic Community

Green burial is not merely a trend driven by environmental concerns; it also resonates deeply with cultural and religious beliefs. One prominent example of this is the growing acceptance of green burial within the Catholic community (Webster, n.d.).

Traditionally, Catholic burial rites have included embalming and the use of ornate caskets, showing respect for the deceased and the holiness of the afterlife. However, in recent years, there has been a noticeable shift among Catholics toward adopting green burial methods.

This transition is based on an understanding of the basic connection between religious ideals and environmental responsibility. Many Catholics regard green burial as a way to honor both their faith's teachings and their dedication to protecting the planet for future generations. By opting for green burial, they can adhere to church doctrine while also embracing eco-friendly burial practices.

What's particularly noteworthy is that numerous Catholic cemeteries now offer green burial options (Markoe, 2014). This indicates the Church's willingness to adjust old practices in response to changing societal ideals and environmental concerns. It's a tangible manifestation of the Church's recognition of the importance of environmental sustainability, and it's an indication of one's commitment to being a responsible steward of the Earth.

Furthermore, the Catholic community's support of green burial is consistent with a broader trend among religious institutions worldwide. Many religious leaders and congregations are recognizing the moral need for environmental stewardship and are working to incorporate eco-friendly practices into their rituals and traditions.

Ultimately, Catholic acceptance of green burial extends beyond pragmatism to develop a deeper spiritual relationship with the natural world. It serves as a reminder that our relationship with the Earth is more than just preservation; it includes reverence and respect for the magnificent creation that surrounds us. By selecting green burial, Catholics not only honor their deceased but also demonstrate their dedication to living in harmony with nature.

As there is an increased awareness in society of environmental concerns, the acceptance and understanding of green burial practices is on the rise. People are recognizing the importance of reducing their ecological footprint even after death, and green burial provides the perfect way to do so. It is a reflection of our changing attitudes toward the planet and our responsibility to preserve it for future generations.

In the next chapter, we will explore another alternative to traditional burial methods: aquamation. This new process, also known as alkaline hydrolysis, offers a novel approach to ecologically acceptable burial solutions, further expanding the options available to those seeking sustainable end-of-life practices.

Chapter 6:

Aquamation

Aquamation, also known as alkaline hydrolysis, is more than simply another funeral choice; it represents a paradigm shift in how we handle the final disposition of our loved ones' remains. Unlike traditional cremation (which uses high heat) or burial (which returns the dead to the earth), aquamation uses water-based technology to gently degrade organic molecules. As we delve into the chapter on aquamation, we will explore its historical roots, environmental benefits, and growing acceptance in modern society.

Historical Background

Origins of Aquamation

In 1888, Amos Herbert Hanson, a British farmer with a propensity for inventiveness, was confronted with a common challenge of the time: what to do with the bodies of deceased farm animals (TalkDeath, 2021). In the late 19th century, the disposal of animal carcasses posed a considerable difficulty for farmers such as Hanson, as old techniques were often inefficient and unhygienic. It was in this context that Hanson's ingenuity led him to a groundbreaking solution that would revolutionize the handling of organic waste.

Hanson embarked on a journey of experimentation, seeking a more effective means of disposing of animal remains while simultaneously harnessing their inherent nutrients. His experiments led him to a remarkable discovery: By immersing the carcasses in a solution of water and potassium hydroxide, commonly referred to as lye, he could speed up the decomposition process. This innovative approach triggered a chemical reaction that effectively broke down the organic matter, transforming it into a nutrient-rich byproduct.

What set Hanson's method apart was its simplicity and effectiveness. By harnessing the power of alkaline hydrolysis, he not only accelerated the decomposition of animal remains but also unlocked the possibility of converting them into a valuable resource: fertilizer (Benson, n.d.). This dual-purpose method addressed both the requirement for effective waste disposal and the aim to capitalize on the intrinsic nutrients found in corpses.

Hanson's pioneering efforts signaled the beginning of what would eventually be known as aquamation, also known as alkaline hydrolysis. Although his initial trials were small-scale, their impact would extend well beyond his farm. Hanson's novel concept gained attention from both agricultural communities and scientific circles, setting the framework for further exploration and refinement of the aquamation process.

Early Uses in Agriculture and Laboratory Settings

Following its serendipitous discovery by Hanson, aquamation quickly found application in a variety of agricultural and laboratory contexts, altering the way organic waste was treated. In agricultural contexts, farmers faced the constant difficulty of efficiently disposing of animal remains while minimizing environmental impact. Traditional methods frequently raised sanitation concerns and failed to maximize the value of animal carcasses.

However, aquamation emerged as a game changer, providing a solution that addressed both sanitation and environmental issues. By submerging animal carcasses in a water and potassium hydroxide solution, farmers could accelerate the decomposition process, transforming organic matter into a valuable fertilizer. This not only reduced the possibility of contamination but also provided farmers with a low-cost method of increasing soil fertility, effectively closing the loop on waste management in agriculture.

In laboratory environments, where the disposal of biohazardous waste presented a significant challenge, aquamation proved to be a safe and effective solution. Contaminated animal bodies, which posed risks to both human health and the environment, could be effectively treated using this technique, which lowered the danger of disease transmission and environmental contamination. The ability of aquamation to break down organic material thoroughly and hygienically made it a popular approach for treating hazardous waste, in accordance with biosafety and environmental stewardship principles.

Aquamation Technology Evolution

Today, modern aquamation machines represent the pinnacle of technological innovation in the field of final disposition. These innovative machines are equipped with advanced features like precise temperature and pressure controls, which ensure that the dissolution of organic material occurs under optimal conditions. By carefully controlling these parameters, aquamation technicians can perform a thorough and efficient body decomposition, resulting in sterile liquid and bone remains.

One of the most significant advances in aquamation technology is its increased energy efficiency and lower environmental impact. Modern machines use sophisticated control systems to function with low energy use while producing outstanding output. This not only lowers operating costs but also minimizes the carbon footprint of the process, making aquamation a greener alternative to traditional cremation methods.

Furthermore, developments in safety measures and regulatory compliance have contributed significantly to aquamation's widespread acceptance in the funeral industry. Rigorous standards ensure that the technique's facilities follow stringent requirements for handling and processing human remains, ensuring the utmost respect and dignity for the deceased and their families.

The Aquamation Process

Aquamation offers a serene and eco-conscious alternative to traditional cremation and burial. Let's take a closer look at the fascinating procedure underlying this novel way of final disposition (Eterneva, n.d.):

- **Setting the stage:** The process begins with the gentle placement of the deceased in a stainless steel vessel. This vessel, which resembles a calm water tank, becomes the stage for the transformation that follows.

- **The elemental alchemy:** As the vessel is filled with water, a crucial element is introduced: potassium hydroxide, often referred to as lye. Despite its unassuming look, this odorless substance performs an important role in the breakdown of organic material. The mixture comprises 95% water and 5% alkali, carefully calibrated to ensure optimal conditions for the process.

- **Harnessing the elements:** Once the vessel is filled, it's time to apply the gentle touch of heat. Temperatures ranging from 200 to 320 degrees Fahrenheit (93 to 160 degrees Celsius) are meticulously controlled to create a warm and nurturing environment. The use of agitation promotes a steady flow, minimizing boiling and aiding the gradual breakdown of organic material.

- **Nature's processes:** Within the vessel, a complex series of biochemical reactions occurs. Fats, proteins, minerals, and carbohydrates undergo decomposition, gradually breaking down into their elemental components. This process mirrors nature's cycles but is hastened by human inventiveness.

- **The essence of transformation:** As the process continues, an incredible change occurs. What was once a physical form has undergone a radical transformation, disintegrating into a sterile green-brown liquid. This liquid, which demonstrates the alchemical power of water and alkali, contains the essence of the deceased.

- **Respecting the cycle:** Just as nature cycles, so does the aquamation process. When the transformation is complete, the liquid is respectfully discharged from the vessel. But the process does not end there. The residual bone material is gently cleansed with fresh water to prepare it for its next phase of existence.

- **Honoring the remains:** Even in its transformed state, the essence of the deceased survives. The bone material, now rendered into a fine powder, is collected with care. It is a tangible memento of a life once lived, waiting to be reunited with family and friends in a solemn act of remembrance.

- **A sustainable legacy:** Beyond its transformative power, aquamation stands out for its minimal environmental impact. Unlike traditional cremation, which emits harmful greenhouse gases and uses fossil fuels, aquamation leaves no such trace. Instead, it represents a lasting legacy that honors both the deceased and the earth we call home.

Commercial Adoption and Regulatory Landscape

First Commercial Aquamation at Albany Medical College

The introduction of the first commercial aquamation machine at Albany Medical College in 1993 was a watershed moment in the history of corpse disposition techniques (Shandilya, 2022). This event was notable because it established aquamation as a commercially feasible alternative to traditional burial and cremation processes.

Motivated by the need for more sustainable and environmentally friendly solutions for dealing with human remains, Albany Medical College installed the aquamation machine to investigate a novel method for final disposition. This pioneering installation cleared the way for this strategy's commercial adoption by demonstrating its practicality and usefulness in a real-world situation. As news spread about this innovative method of body disposal, it sparked interest among funeral industry experts and the general public, prompting further exploration and investment in this final disposition technology.

However, the introduction of aquamation was not without its challenges. Initial reactions from the public and industry stakeholders were mixed, with some expressing skepticism or worry about this unusual procedure. Questions concerning aquamation's safety, efficacy, and ethical implications arose, necessitating education and outreach efforts to address concerns and misconceptions.

Cost-Effective Animal Commercial Use

Aquamation emerged as a game-changer in the realm of animal disposal, offering a practical and economical solution for veterinary settings (DaySmart Vet, 2022). Traditionally, the alternatives for dealing with deceased animals were limited and often costly. However, aquamation offered a groundbreaking alternative that revolutionized the way veterinarians handled animal remains.

Unlike traditional cremation methods, which require significant energy expenditure and maintenance of high-temperature furnaces, aquamation offers a more efficient and environmentally friendly approach. By using a water-based process and lower temperatures, aquamation reduces energy consumption and operating costs, making it an appealing choice for veterinarians wishing to manage their budgets while maintaining high standards of care.

Furthermore, aquamation's mild procedure appealed to veterinary specialists who value ethical and humane treatment of animals, even in death. The method's emphasis on natural decomposition, aided by water and alkalinity, appealed to individuals looking for a more courteous and environmentally conscientious approach to animal waste. Rather than subjecting animal remains to high temperatures and flames, aquamation provided a quiet and dignified option that was consistent with veterinarians' dedication to the welfare of animals.

Nevertheless, despite its numerous advantages, the use of aquamation for animals has not been without criticism. Some individuals and organizations have expressed ethical concerns about the disposal of animal remains, questioning if aquamation adequately respects the dignity of dead animals. Furthermore, issues have emerged concerning the disposal of aquamation byproducts, particularly the resulting liquid waste and its potential. environmental impact.

However, proponents hold the opinion that aquamation is a huge step forward in promoting sustainable and humane veterinary care procedures. It has transformed veterinarians' approach to end-of-life care for their beloved animal patients by providing a cost-effective, environmentally friendly, and compassionate alternative to traditional methods of animal disposal, paving the way for a more ethical and sustainable future in veterinary medicine.

Minnesota's Pioneering Approval of Aquamation

In 2003, Minnesota made history by becoming the first state in the United States to legalize aquamation for human use in funeral ceremonies (McGee, 2023). This decision marked a significant milestone in the evolution of end-of-life options and funeral industry practices.

The approval of aquamation in Minnesota didn't come without careful consideration and regulatory review. Legislative and regulatory processes were carried out to assess the safety, efficacy, and ethical implications of this innovative approach to body disposition. Experts from a variety of professions, including medical, environmental science, and funeral services, have had a role in the aquamation approval process.

The significance of Minnesota's approval cannot be overemphasized. It marked a movement in the funeral business toward more ecologically conscious and sustainable practices. By formally recognizing aquamation as a valid alternative to traditional burial and cremation, Minnesota set a precedent for other states to follow.

Following Minnesota's pioneering permission, aquamation gained popularity in the funeral industry. The state's funeral homes and crematoriums began offering aquamation to families looking for alternatives to traditional burial or cremation. The adoption of this method marked a diversification of services within the funeral industry, giving consumers more options for end-of-life arrangements.

The impact of aquamation's adoption in Minnesota extended beyond state borders. It spurred discussion and interest in other areas regarding the possible advantages of this flameless cremation procedure. Funeral directors, environmental activists, and individuals implementing end-of-life arrangements began looking into this final disposition option as a sustainable and environmentally friendly solution.

Variations in State Regulations

Aquamation regulations vary by state, reflecting a broad terrain of attitudes and concerns across the United States (Keene, n.d.). While some states have welcomed this option to traditional burial and cremation, others have imposed limits, often asserting environmental and logistical concerns.

In states where aquamation is permitted, approval processes and requirements often vary. These can range from specific licensing for facilities to guidelines on waste disposal and water usage. States may also differ in how they oversee and supervise aquamation facilities to ensure compliance with health and safety standards.

However, not all states have embraced aquamation with open arms. Some have established bans or limitations, particularly in areas where water scarcity is a major concern. Aquamation uses a lot of water, which raises concerns about its long-term viability in arid climates or drought-prone areas. States may choose to regulate aquamation to reduce potential strain on water supplies and infrastructure.

These regulatory considerations have a direct impact on aquamation's availability as an end-of-life option for individuals in various locations. Individuals in states where it is prohibited or strongly controlled might have limited access to this alternative means of disposal. This can restrict choices for those seeking environmentally friendly options or alternatives to traditional burial and cremation.

The ongoing debate surrounding the environmental sustainability of aquamation affects future regulatory developments. As technology progresses and concerns about climate change grow, there may be an increased need to address the environmental impact of end-of-life practices. This could lead to further scrutiny and possibly modifications to aquamation legislation, aiming to balance environmental concerns with individual choice and accessibility.

Environmental Impact and Benefits

Aquamation vs. Traditional Cremation and Burial

Aquamation provides a substantial advancement in ecologically sensitive end-of-life solutions when compared to standard cremation and burial techniques (Gonzales, 2021). When we think of cremation, we might envision billowing smoke rising from a chimney. While this technology is often used, it's not without its environmental consequences. Cremation emits carbon dioxide and other pollutants into the atmosphere, which contribute to air pollution and climate change. The enormous amount of cremations worldwide implies that these pollutants can accumulate quickly, worsening environmental concerns.

Aquamation, on the other hand, runs without combustion, meaning it does not produce any of these harmful emissions. Instead, it uses a water-based process to gradually break down the body's organic matter, leaving behind only bone fragments and a sterile liquid. This liquid is safe to be discharged into wastewater systems, and it can even be used to nourish plants, making it a sustainable alternative to the smoke and ash produced during cremation.

Burial, while a more traditional option, has its ecological challenges. Traditional burials necessitate the use of land for gravesites, which destroys habitats. If not managed effectively, this method can contribute to groundwater contamination. Additionally, the materials used in caskets and burial vaults can take years to decompose, further adding to the environmental impact.

Therefore, under these circumstances, aquamation provides a cleaner, greener alternative, speeding up the natural decomposition process without releasing any hazardous substances. This delicate, eco-friendly approach appeals to people who want to reduce their environmental impact even in death.

Looking ahead, the next chapter introduces another innovative approach to final disposition: tree pod burial. This eco-friendly alternative offers a unique way to reconnect with nature and contribute to the growth of new life. Read on as we dig into the concept of tree pod burial and explore its potential to transform our relationship with death and the environment.

Chapter 7:

Tree Pod Burial

In this chapter, we will look at the innovative concept of tree pod burials, a unique burial system that intertwines the cycle of life and nature. Tree pod burials encompass planting a tree alongside or atop a biodegradable urn containing a person's remains, promoting the growth of new life from the old. We'll look at both the conceptual roots of this practice and the practical possibilities accessible today, allowing you to consider the profound relationship between life, death, and the natural world.

Overview of the Concept of Tree Pod Burials

Tree pod burials offer a heartfelt and eco-conscious alternative to honor deceased family and friends beyond the traditional methods of burial or cremation. Imagine a peaceful forest or garden, where instead of headstones, vibrant trees stand tall, each one a living tribute to someone cherished. This is the essence of tree pod burials: a magnificent fusion of human legacy and the natural world.

Unlike conventional burial practices that often involve embalming chemicals or cremation processes releasing carbon emissions, tree pod burials have a low environmental impact. The concept represents a deep connection between life and death, as nature's cycle continues uninterrupted. Families take comfort in knowing that their loved ones contribute to the growth of new life, leaving a legacy that lasts well beyond their lifetime on Earth. Tree pod funerals provide more than simply a final resting place; they are a profound reminder of the interdependence of all living things, leaving a legacy of love and sustainability for future generations.

The Birth of an Eco-Friendly Legacy: Capsula Mundi

In 2016, the world of burial practices witnessed a revolutionary idea take root with the unveiling of the *Tree Pod Burial System*, developed by Italian designers Francesco D'Angelo and Adriano Del Ferro (Research for Life, n.d.). Dubbed Capsula Mundi, meaning "world's capsule", this original concept sought to redefine the way we bid farewell to our family and friends, offering a sustainable and environmentally conscious alternative to traditional burial methods.

At its core, Capsula Mundi represents a significant shift from traditional burial practices by introducing a concept that recognizes the intrinsic connection between life and nature. While the original idea of encapsulating the full body in a biodegradable pod remains conceptual for now, the present product is a biodegradable urn designed to hold the remains of the deceased (Better Place

Forests, n.d.-d). A newly planted tree is put alongside or atop this caring embrace, symbolizing life's continuity and the interdependence of all living beings.

The beauty of Capsula Mundi lies not only in its practicality but also in its poetic symbolism. The concept develops a profound connection between people and nature by linking the deceased's journey with the growth of a living tree. It symbolizes the eternal cycle of life, death, and rebirth, providing peace and comfort to both the deceased and their loved ones.

D'Angelo and Del Ferro's Capsula Mundi is more than just a burial option; it is also a means of leaving a permanent legacy that will be passed down through generations. By selecting this end-of-life choice, we not only commemorate the memory of people we have lost but also plant the seeds for a greener, more sustainable future.

Visualizing the Burial Process

The burial process begins with the gentle placement of the deceased's ashes within a biodegradable pod, evocative of a cocoon or seed, symbolizing the potential for new life (Ever Loved, 2024). This pod is then respectfully buried in the ground, either beside an existing tree or as the foundation for a new tree planting. In the latter situation, a young sapling is carefully placed right above the buried pod, symbolizing life's interdependence and the seamless transition between existence and renewal.

As the seasons unfold and time passes, the biodegradable pod gradually decomposes, blending in with the soil and restoring the individual's remains to their elemental state. In this transformational process, the nutrients released from the decomposing pod nourish the growing tree's roots, increasing its strength and vigor. This deep symbiosis between the departed and the tree encapsulates the endless cycle of life, death, and regeneration, confirming the interconnectedness of all living species within the intricate web of nature.

When loved ones visit the site, they see a tangible representation of their treasured memories taking root and blossoming alongside the growing tree. Each visit provides an opportunity for reflection, celebration, and connection, as the tree is a living homage to the departed's enduring legacy. Through this profound union of human and arboreal life, the tree pod burial system not only honors the memory of the deceased but also bestows upon them a timeless and enduring legacy that resonates across the natural world.

Environmental Benefits and Symbolism

The tree pod burial system has significant environmental benefits. By using biodegradable materials for the pod and integrating burial sites into natural landscapes, the concept reduces the ecological impact of traditional burial practices. Instead of taking up valuable ground in cemeteries, these burial places serve as biodiversity sanctuaries, encouraging the emergence of a diverse plant and animal population.

Furthermore, the trees planted in conjunction with these burials serve an important part in mitigating the effects of climate change. As they grow, they absorb carbon dioxide from the atmosphere, which helps to reduce greenhouse gas emissions and improve air quality. In effect, each tree serves as a living memorial, maintaining the memory of the fallen while also contributing to the planet's health and sustainability.

In embracing this type of burial system, individuals can find solace in knowing that their loved ones' legacies will live on through the flourishing of nature. It's a profound way to honor the past while also nurturing the future, ensuring that future generations inherit a world enriched by the love and memory of those who came before them.

Current Options

Global Capsula Mundi Limitations

Despite its innovative premise, the Capsula Mundi burial technique has not been widely adopted worldwide. This is primarily due to logistical issues and regulatory complications. While many people find the thought of being buried in a fetal position under a tree to be both environmentally and emotionally desirable, making this a reality has proven to be quite challenging.

One major obstacle is navigating the myriad of regulations and laws surrounding burial practices in different regions. Furthermore, the logistical constraints of mass-producing and distributing Capsula Mundi pods have presented considerable challenges. As a result, the availability of Capsula Mundi remains limited, leaving many intrigued but unable to access this innovative burial option.

However, the growing demand for eco-friendly burial alternatives has led to the development of alternative options, providing individuals with similar opportunities to leave a sustainable legacy. One such alternative is "The Living Urn by Biolife" (The Living Urn, 2015), which provides a practical and accessible solution to tree pod burials. "The Living Urn" incorporates cremated ashes into a biodegradable urn with a section for planting a tree, allowing individuals to contribute to the growth of a tree in their honor.

This biodegradable urn securely holds the ashes, serving as a nurturing vessel for a young tree seed or sapling. As the tree grows, it becomes a living memorial, offering peace and comfort to those who seek its shade.

What distinguishes "The Living Urn" is its simplicity and versatility. Whether planted in a backyard garden, a neighborhood park, or a favorite natural setting, each tree becomes a symbol of hope and rejuvenation. Families are encouraged to actively participate in the growth process, building a stronger connection to both nature and their deceased loved one.

In a world where environmental consciousness is increasingly valued, "The Living Urn" offers a fitting tribute that is consistent with personal beliefs and values. It exemplifies the circle of life, in which death gives way to new beginnings, and memories are forever intertwined with the beauty of nature.

Eco-Friendly Memorial Growth

The functionality of "The Living Urn" offers a heartfelt and eco-conscious way to honor a loved one's memory while contributing to the environment. Look upon it as a special vessel, made with both reverence and innovation.

First, this biodegradable urn provides a secure and dignified container for your loved one's cremated remains. Its design guarantees that the ashes are safely contained, allowing for a peaceful transfer into nature's embrace.

Nestled within the urn is a unique compartment specifically crafted for planting a tree seed or sapling. It's almost as if you're giving your loved one a fresh start. This seed or sapling becomes the centerpiece of a living memorial, representing growth, rebirth, and the endless cycle of life.

The urn decomposes with time, merging harmoniously with the soil. This process isn't just symbolic but also practical. The decomposition of the urn releases vital nutrients into the soil, nourishing the budding tree. The remains of your loved one form a wonderful synergy with the flourishing life of the tree.

What's truly remarkable is Biolife's patented system for ensuring optimal tree-growing conditions. From soil composition to moisture levels, every detail is carefully considered to enhance sustainability and longevity. This means that your chosen tree has the best possible chance to thrive, creating a lasting legacy that can be cherished for generations to come.

Choosing the Right Tree

Several variables should be carefully addressed when selecting the most suitable tree species (Better Place Forests, n.d.-c). To begin, determine the climate suitability of the chosen location for planting the tree. Different trees thrive in different climates, so choose one that can adapt to the local weather conditions.

Additionally, understanding the growth characteristics of the tree is essential. For instance, some trees may have expansive canopies or stunning blossoms. Consider how the tree's growth pattern and appearance relate to the desired aesthetic and symbolism for the burial site.

Personal preferences also play a major role in selecting the tree. Whether it's a favorite tree species, one with personal importance, or a tree noted for its ecological benefits, the choice should be special for the individual or family.

When calculating costs, it is important to consider more than simply the price of the burial pod. The budget should cover the selected tree species, its size, and any additional services needed, such as planting assistance or care. Costs can vary depending on location, supplier, and any customization options chosen.

By carefully considering these factors and evaluating the accompanying costs, individuals can ensure that their tree pod burial honors their memory in a way that is both environmentally sustainable and deeply meaningful. Whether it's providing shade for future generations or helping local ecosystems, the choice of tree can leave a lasting legacy of love and respect.

Practical Considerations and Logistics

Cost Analysis

When considering a tree pod burial, it's necessary to understand the various aspects that contribute to the overall cost. Here's a breakdown to help you plan more effectively:

Explanation of Cost Range

The cost of a tree burial pod varies greatly based on numerous criteria. To begin, the cost will be determined by the type of pod you purchase. Some pods may be simple in appearance, while others may include more elaborate craftsmanship or customization choices, which can increase the price. Additionally, the chosen tree species plays a significant role. Some of these species may be more expensive or harder to source than others. Finally, geographical location also affects the cost, as prices may differ between regions due to factors such as the availability of materials and local market conditions.

Breakdown of Costs

The cost of a tree burial pod varies depending on the vendor and the type of tree selected, including where you buy the tree itself (The Living Urn, 2021). Prices can range from $129 to upwards of $400. Numerous funeral homes across the nation offer "Living Urn" tree burial pods, which are also available for online purchase. In addition, while some individuals opt for the complete package including both the burial pod and a young tree from "The Living Urn," others may choose to purchase only the pod system and acquire a sapling separately from a nearby nursery. These prices may also vary based on your location and the availability of specific options in your area.

Considerations for Budgeting

When budgeting for a tree pod burial, you must examine how the expense fits into your overall financial plan. Begin by examining your budget and determining how much you're willing to spend on this item. Keep in mind that, while a tree pod burial may be a meaningful alternative, you must compare it against other funeral or memorial options to ensure it corresponds with your values and financial resources. Consider contacting companies for estimates and investigating several options to discover the best match for your budget and preferences.

Options for Acquiring Burial Pods and Trees

When considering a tree pod burial, you have two main options for obtaining the necessary components: purchasing through specialized companies like The Living Urn or sourcing them from local nurseries.

Purchasing Through the Living Urn

If you choose to work with firms like The Living Urn, the process is simple. You can visit their website or contact them directly to explore their range of burial pod options and tree selections. These companies often offer a variety of customization options, allowing you to personalize the burial pod with engravings or select from different tree species based on your preferences or the environment in which the tree will be planted. Once you've made your selections, the company will handle the ordering process and arrange for delivery to your specified location. This option offers convenience and peace of mind because you can rely on the specialized providers' experience to ensure that everything is handled professionally.

Local Nurseries

Alternatively, you can choose to purchase a burial pod separately and procure a tree from local nurseries or tree farms in your area. This option has the benefit of supporting local businesses while also allowing you to explore a broader range of tree species that may be more suited to your climate and soil type. Visiting local nurseries allows you to personally inspect the trees before making a decision, ensuring that you get a healthy and sturdy specimen. While this option may require a little more effort than purchasing through specialized companies, it can be a rewarding experience that allows you to actively participate in your local community and environment.

Whether you choose to purchase through established companies or support local nurseries, both alternatives provide an opportunity to realize your dream of a tree pod burial, allowing you to pay a meaningful and environmentally conscious tribute to your loved one.

Legal Aspect

When considering a tree pod burial on private land, it is imperative to understand the legal framework governing such procedures (VanderVaate, 2023). Rules and regulations for burial and interment vary by state, even on private land. Understanding these rules is crucial for ensuring compliance and avoiding potential legal concerns down the line. Some states may impose special burial regulations or restrictions, such as burial depth, the use of burial containers, and environmental issues.

Furthermore, getting permits or authorization from local authorities may be required before performing a tree burial on private property. These permits verify that the burial process follows local standards and poses no environmental or public health hazards. Local government authorities or departments in charge of land use and zoning can typically provide guidance on how to get such permissions.

Property owners should also examine the legal repercussions of interring remains on their property. This includes understanding their property rights, any applicable zoning regulations, and any future ramifications for property sales or transfers. While many property owners are drawn to the notion of a tree pod burial, it is important to thoroughly explore the legal implications.

As we contemplate the potential impact of tree pod burials, it's important to recognize the opportunity they offer to leave a lasting impression on the world. Individuals who choose this burial option can leave behind not only memories but tangible contributions to the environment, nurturing the growth of a tree that will serve as a living tribute to their life.

Furthermore, watching a tree grow in memory of a loved one is incredibly meaningful. It transforms into a living sign of the loved one's presence, providing consolation and comfort to all who visit and reflect beneath its branches. Each leaf, branch, and flower becomes a treasured memento of the person buried beneath its roots, thus forging a lasting bond.

Let us now explore yet another option in environmentally friendly burial practices: terramation. In the coming chapter, we will explore the innovative concept of terramation and its potential to revolutionize the way we approach end-of-life preparations. Turn the page to learn about this fascinating topic and continue our quest for more sustainable and meaningful ways to honor our loved ones.

Chapter 8:

Terramation

Terramation represents an innovative way of burial that differs from traditional methods such as green burials. This novel procedure, also known as human composting, converts bodies into nutrient-rich soil, which appeals to ardent gardeners looking for a sustainable afterlife solution. As we delve into the complexities of terramation, we'll look at technological advancements, legal status, and the powerful emotional resonance it has for individuals and families alike.

Understanding Terramation

Terramation differs from typical burial procedures in that it provides a unique and environmentally friendly method of treating human remains. Terramation is the controlled decomposition of a deceased person to create organic soil. Unlike traditional burials, where bodies are interred intact or cremated into ashes, terramation harnesses natural decomposition to return the deceased to the earth in a beneficial way.

This practice is in sharp contrast to green burials, which stress minimal environmental effects by avoiding embalming fluids and non-biodegradable materials. While green burials involve burying the body in natural cloth or a biodegradable container to aid decomposition, terramation takes the idea a step further by actively transforming the body into the soil. This contrast is both practical and philosophical, as terramation highlights the cyclical nature of life and death, with bodies playing an important role in the earth's regeneration.

For gardening enthusiasts, the appeal of terramation lies in the opportunity to cultivate new life from the remains of their loved ones. Consider the profound connection of tending a garden nurtured by soil infused with the essence of those who have passed away. It provides a real means to respect their memory and carry on their legacy, transforming loss into development and rebirth. Furthermore, the possibility of making a meaningful contribution to the ecosystem appeals strongly to people who value sustainability and environmental care.

Ultimately, terramation is essentially a peaceful merger of life and death, providing a sustainable alternative to traditional burial procedures. It appeals not only to the environmentally aware but also to those who find solace in the concept of physically reconnecting to the soil.

The Process of Terramation

Sealed Chamber Composting

Terramation initiates within a sealed chamber, carefully designed to facilitate the decomposition process while minimizing any potential discomfort or odor (The Natural Funeral, n.d.). This sealed enclosure provides a regulated setting for the transformation of human remains into nutrient-rich soil.

Air Filtration System

The advanced air filtration system included within the sealed chamber is essential to the terramation process's success. This filtration system guarantees that gases produced by the natural decomposition of organic matter, such as carbon dioxide and methane, are adequately handled. This careful filtration procedure not only maintains a pleasant environment within the chamber but also ensures compliance with stringent regulatory criteria for dealing with humans.

Odor Elimination

One of the key concerns in composting human remains is the possibility of unpleasant odors. However, with developments in terramation technology, odor removal has become a top priority. The sealed chamber, together with the air filtering system, efficiently contains and neutralizes any odors that may occur during the composting process. This ensures that both the dignity of the deceased and the comfort of those overseeing the process are respected throughout the entire terramation procedure.

Duration and Stages

The terramation process is divided into steps, each precisely planned to promote the efficient breakdown of human remains while increasing the quality of the resulting soil (Recompose, n.d.). Understanding the duration and complexities of these stages is essential to understanding the overall process of terramation.

Initial Composting Phase (5 to 7 Weeks)

During the early composting phase, the sealed chamber creates a perfect environment for microbial activity to flourish. As the body decomposes in this regulated environment, organic matter degrades into its basic elements, releasing vital nutrients into the surrounding environment. Over the course of four to seven weeks, this active decomposition process converts the corpse into compost, a nutrient-rich substance. Throughout this phase, the air filtration system meticulously maintains optimal conditions within the chamber, ensuring efficient decomposition while minimizing any potential odors.

Curing Phase (3 to 5 Weeks)

Following the initial composting phase, the resulting product goes through a curing procedure to improve its quality and stability. The compost is transferred to an aerated bin and left to mature for three to five weeks. During this time, microbial activity continues to degrade any leftover organic waste, allowing the compost to stabilize and reach its optimal nutrient content. The careful management of environmental variables, such as temperature and moisture levels, ensures that the compost reaches the desired quality for future use.

Environmental Benefits

Individuals who choose terramation as an end-of-life option not only satisfy the wishes of their deceased for a natural afterlife but also take an active role in preserving the environment for future generations. Through the sustainable transformation of human remains into nutrient-rich soil, terramation offers a meaningful way to honor the cycle of life while contributing to the preservation and restoration of the natural world. Here are some of the benefits offered by this life disposition option:

- **Reduced environmental impact:** Terramation offers a sustainable alternative to traditional burial and cremation procedures, which often involve resources like embalming fluids, caskets, and fossil fuels. By diverting human remains from these conventional practices, terramation helps minimize the carbon footprint associated with end-of-life rituals.

- **Promotion of ecosystem health:** Terramation produces nutrient-rich soil that has the potential to improve local ecosystems. When used to improve soil quality, this compost can promote plant growth, improve soil structure, and increase biodiversity. By returning essential nutrients to the earth in a natural and beneficial manner, terramation supports the health and resilience of surrounding ecosystems.

- **Support for sustainable agriculture:** In addition to its environmental benefits, terramation compost is an important resource for sustainable farming techniques. When mixed into agricultural fields, this nutrient-rich soil can increase crop yields, minimize the demand for synthetic fertilizers, and improve soil health. By contributing to sustainable farming methods, terramation aligns with efforts to safeguard food security and promote environmental stewardship.

- **Preservation of natural resources:** Terramation preserves natural resources by reducing the demand for land, energy, and materials associated with traditional burial and cremation techniques. By converting human remains into an environmentally beneficial resource, terramation exemplifies a circular approach to end-of-life care, wherein the natural cycles of life and death are honored and celebrated.

Embracing terramation allows individuals to leave a meaningful legacy of environmental responsibility. Individuals who choose a sustainable afterlife option not only honor their own values and beliefs but also encourage future generations to prioritize environmental protection and stewardship. In this way, terramation becomes not only a personal choice but also a powerful statement of commitment to the preservation and restoration of the natural world for generations to come.

Ethical and Religious Perspectives

Examination of Ethical Implications

When considering the practice of terramation, or human composting, a range of ethical questions naturally arise. These questions address topics such as respect for the deceased, environmental sustainability, and cultural traditions surrounding death and burial.

One key ethical consideration is the treatment of human remains. Terramation advocates say that it is a more respectful and environmentally responsible alternative to traditional burial or cremation. They believe that returning the body to the earth in the form of nutrient-rich soil honors the natural cycle of life and death. However, some may raise concerns about the dignity of the deceased and whether the process of composting properly respects their memory.

Furthermore, there are ethical issues for consent and autonomy. Advocates emphasize the necessity of allowing people to choose their preferred mode of disposition for their remains, whether it is traditional burial, cremation, or terramation. Ensuring informed consent and respecting the deceased's wishes are fundamental ethical considerations in end-of-life care.

Perspectives From Different Religious Traditions

Religious beliefs and traditions often influence how people handle death and burial. Terramation perspectives vary widely among different religious traditions.

In Christianity, for example, views on terramation may differ depending on denominational interpretations of burial rituals and afterlife beliefs (McDonald, 2023). Some Christian denominations may regard terramation as a way to honor the land and promote environmental stewardship, which aligns with their theology. Others may have qualms due to traditional beliefs about the sanctity of the body and the resurrection of the dead.

Similarly, other religious traditions such as Islam, Judaism, Hinduism, and Buddhism have their own perspectives on death and burial. These perspectives are influenced by religious texts, cultural practices, and theological concepts. For example, in Islam, there are precise recommendations for how to treat the deceased respectfully, including prompt burial. Cremation is a prevalent practice in Hinduism, reflecting beliefs about the natural cycle of life and rebirth.

Addressing Concerns and Encouraging Dialogue

Given the diverse viewpoints on terramation, it is important to address concerns and engage in constructive dialogue. This involves open communication among advocates, religious leaders, ethicists, and the general public.

One prevalent worry is that terramation may be perceived as disrespectful or undignified. To address this, advocates underline the cautious and respectful nature of the composting process, which is carried out in a controlled atmosphere while adhering to hygiene and safety regulations.

Engaging with religious communities is also important for promoting understanding and dialogue. Advocates can identify common ground and resolve any concerns or objections by respecting religious beliefs and traditions, as well as accepting varied perspectives.

Legal Acceptance

Terramation, as a novel approach to handling human remains, has acquired considerable attention in both legal and cultural spheres. Understanding its existing legal status, growing support, and regional availability offers insight into the evolving landscape of end-of-life practices.

Current Legal Status

Terramation is currently legal in several states in the United States, including Washington, California, Oregon, Colorado, Nevada, Vermont, and New York (Team Earth, 2022). However, the legal framework surrounding terramation continues to evolve, with ongoing legislative attempts aimed at increasing its availability to other regions. Despite differences in state regulations, the overall trend indicates a rising acceptance of terramation as a viable alternative to traditional burial and cremation practices.

Growing Support and Legislative Progress

Support for terramation is steadily gaining momentum, driven by a combination of environmental concerns, shifting cultural attitudes, and a desire for more sustainable end-of-life options (Houser, 2022). Legislative proposals aimed at legalizing terramation in states where it is now illegal or unregulated reflect this growing support. Advocacy groups and grassroots initiatives that promote terramation as a respectful and environmentally friendly alternative to traditional burial practices further contribute to its increasing acceptance within society.

Regional Availability

While terramation is legal in certain states, its availability may vary depending on local regulations and the presence of facilities equipped to perform the procedure. Individuals interested in using terramation as an end-of-life option should check with local authorities and funeral service providers to see if it is available in their area. Furthermore, continuous legislative efforts and rising public awareness may lead to increased availability of terramation services in the future, making them available to a greater part of the population looking for sustainable and ecologically conscientious alternatives for final disposition.

Cost Analysis

When considering end-of-life arrangements, financial considerations often play a significant role in decision-making. Terramation, while providing a unique and environmentally friendly alternative to traditional burial and cremation, has its own set of costs.

Terramation costs typically vary based on several factors, including geographical location, service provider, and any additional preferences or services chosen by the individual or their family. Terramation typically costs between $5,000 and $7,000, while pricing might vary depending on local market conditions and individual service offers (Team Earth, 2022).

Compared to traditional burial or cremation, the cost of terramation may initially appear higher. However, it is necessary to evaluate the long-term advantages and potential savings connected with an environmentally beneficial choice. Unlike traditional burial, which often requires the purchase of a casket, burial plot, and other fees, terramation removes many of these expenses. Similarly, terramation eliminates the energy-intensive cremation procedure, which uses a lot of fuel and may incur additional fees for urns and memorial services.

Moreover, the sustainability and environmental benefits of terramation can offer additional value beyond its initial cost. By returning the body to the earth in the form of nutrient-rich soil, terramation promotes ecosystem health and minimizes the carbon footprint associated with conventional burial and cremation practices. For environmentally conscious individuals and families, the long-term ecological impact of terramation may exceed its initial financial investment.

Emotional and Symbolic Significance of Terramation

In the realm of burial practices, the emotional and symbolic significance of terramation goes beyond conventional approaches. From developing a strong personal connection to the environment to encouraging meaningful family involvement and the establishment of memorial gardens, this eco-friendly option appeals to individuals wanting a sustainable and emotionally resonant end-of-life solution.

Personal Connection to the Earth

Terramation cultivates a uniquely personal connection to the environment by allowing everyone to contribute to the cycle of life in a tangible and meaningful way. By embracing the concept of the natural process of decomposition and returning to the soil, individuals find satisfaction in knowing that their remains will nourish the earth and sustain future generations. This sense of connectivity with the environment promotes profound calm and harmony, allowing individuals to leave a lasting legacy based on sustainability and regard for the natural world.

Creation of Memorial Gardens

One of the most appealing characteristics of terramation is its ability to inspire the creation of vivid and peaceful memorial gardens. Unlike traditional burial plots, which often require extensive maintenance and upkeep, memorial gardens provide a peaceful and environmentally friendly final resting place for those we love. These living memorials serve as a tangible tribute to the individuals who have embraced terramation, providing family members and friends with a peaceful sanctuary for reflection and remembrance.

The creation of a memorial garden also provides a creative outlet for expression, allowing families to personalize the space based on their loved one's passions and interests. Whether decorated with native plants, engraved stones, or symbolic sculptures, each garden symbolizes the unique spirit and legacy of the individual whose remains enrich the soil below. As visitors stroll through these tranquil landscapes, they are invited to connect with nature, honor the memories of their loved ones, and find comfort in the beauty of life's eternal cycle.

Family Involvement and Commemoration

Terramation encourages active family involvement throughout the entire process, from the initial decision-making stages to the creation of lasting memorials. Unlike traditional burial and cremation rites, which can feel impersonal or distant, terramation allows families to actively participate in honoring their loved one's legacy and celebrating their life in a meaningful way.

From choosing the location for the memorial garden to engaging in the composting process, families can participate in highly meaningful rituals that respect their dear one's memory and renew their bonds. This collaborative approach to end-of-life care promotes a sense of unity and support within the family, allowing them to find peace and closure during their grieving period.

In essence, terramation is more than simply a disposal method; it is a holistic approach to end-of-life care that honors the individual, celebrates their legacy, and strengthens the bonds of family and community. Individuals and families can find serenity, healing, and connection in the earth's embrace by acknowledging its emotional and symbolic value.

Prospects for the Future

The future of terramation is promising, with increasing legal acceptance and growing public interest (Return Home, 2023). Apart from being currently legalized in several states, bills are being introduced in others, so it is possible that it will become more widely available in the coming years. As awareness of environmental issues continues to grow, more people are seeking alternatives to traditional burial and cremation, making terramation an enticing choice for many.

Furthermore, technological developments and refinement of terramation procedures are expected to increase the practice's efficiency and accessibility. Research on refining composting processes and increasing the environmental benefits of terramation is ongoing, paving the way for a more sustainable future in end-of-life care.

Ultimately, terramation brings solace to loved ones by ensuring that their deceased family member or friend continues to play an important role in the ecosystem. Instead of being buried in a casket or dispersed in the wind, their remnants become part of the land, promoting new life and growth. This holistic approach to death and burial cultivates a deeper connection to the natural world and reinforces the cycle of life.

Moving on, it's worth mentioning that while terramation provides a land-based alternative for eco-conscious burial, there is another option available for people who are drawn to the vastness of the ocean: burial at sea. In the following chapter, we'll explore the rich history and cultural significance of this maritime custom, as well as the practical considerations and environmental implications of burying loved ones beneath the waters. Join us as we travel across the oceans to discover the eternal beauty and solemnity of burial at sea.

Chapter 9:

Burial at Sea

This chapter delves into the intriguing practice of burying loved ones to rest under the vast expanse of ocean waves. We'll take a close look at a true story involving a woman's unconventional wish for a burial at sea. It also explores the historical backdrop and legislative landscape surrounding sea burials, shedding light on the environmental considerations and personal motivations that lead people to choose this unusual farewell.

Death as Life's Culmination

Death is a universal truth, the culmination of the journey we all embark upon from the moment we're born. It's a topic fraught with mystery and dread, but it's an unavoidable aspect of life. How we choose to honor the deceased varies widely between cultures and individuals, with burial, cremation, and more unorthodox rituals such as sea burial offering diverse paths to bid farewell to our beloved family members and friends.

At this point, I'd like to share the moving story of Lois Woodburn, an 85-year-old American woman from Los

Angeles (Pineda, 2023). Lois's journey toward her final resting place exemplifies the uniqueness of human needs and the infinite depths of love that survive even death.

The True Story of Lois Woodburn

Lois decided on an unconventional farewell long before her passing. A commercial artist by profession, she had lived a life colored by creativity, kindness, and a deep appreciation for the beauty of nature, particularly the vast expanse of the ocean.

Years before her death, Lois had expressed her wish for a burial at sea to a mortician she met at a party. She emphatically stated that, when her time came, she wanted her entire body to be consigned to the depths of the ocean. It was to be a final act of surrender to the majestic waves that had long captured her heart.

The Ceremony

As Lois's health began to deteriorate, her daughter Teresa Stremcha found herself faced with the solemn task of honoring her mother's dying wish. So, on August 21, 2022, with unyielding determination, Teresa embarked on a journey to ensure that her beloved mother's farewell would be nothing short of extraordinary. With around 30 family members and friends, they sailed off from Long Beach Harbor, six miles offshore, to say goodbye to their beloved matriarch.

The scene was one of immense beauty and solemnity as the yacht carrying Lois's casket bobbed gently on the azure waters. A second boat, carrying the personnel overseeing the burial, floated alongside, adding to the sense of reverence in the air. As Lois's stainless steel casket was carefully dropped into the ocean's embrace, a hush fell over the gathering, broken only by the soft lapping of waves against the hull.

For Teresa and the rest of Lois's loved ones, the ceremony was a bittersweet blend of sorrow and solace. It was a fitting farewell for a woman who had lived life on her own terms, embracing every opportunity with grace and courage. As they watched the ocean claim Lois's earthly vessel, they took comfort in knowing that she would always be intertwined with the element she cherished most.

Lois found her eternal resting place in the tranquil waters off the coast of Long Beach Harbor, a timeless homage to a life well spent and a love that surpassed the boundaries of mortality. As the sun dipped below the horizon, casting its golden rays over the sea, those gathered on the yacht found solace in the knowledge that Lois's spirit would forever dwell upon the waves she so adored.

Historical and Practical Aspects

Historical Context of Burial at Sea

Burials at sea have a rich history spanning thousands of years and various civilizations (TalkDeath, 2018). Ancient cultures such as the Romans, Greeks, and Egyptians practiced sea burials alongside other funeral traditions. Vikings, known for their maritime skill, performed elaborate "ship burials" in which the deceased was laid to rest in naval vessels that were sometimes set on fire and driven out to sea. The Norse sagas mention pouring ashes over the water and burning ships as funeral rites.

The British developed their own customs, which included sewing bodies into shrouds made from ship materials and holding religious services before the sea burial. These rituals were often reserved for those who died far from home or during battles when traditional land burials were impossible. Sea burials represented a connection between life, death, and the vastness of the ocean, providing a meaningful farewell to loved ones lost at sea.

Modern Practices and Regulations Governing Burial at Sea

In modern times, burial at sea is a solemn and regulated practice. In the United States, for example, the

Environmental Protection Agency (EPA) oversees particular criteria for disposing of human remains in ocean waters (Return Home, 2023b). These regulations ensure that funerals at sea are carried out in an environmentally responsible manner with regard to marine ecosystems and public health.

The Marine Protection, Research, and Sanctuaries Act (MPRSA) establishes guidelines for the transport and burial of human remains in maritime waters (US EPA, 2024). Such burials require permits, which must be obtained under particular criteria. For example, the body should not be embalmed but placed in a biodegradable casket or sewn into a shroud before being carefully lowered into the ocean. Furthermore, burials at sea are forbidden within three nautical miles of shore, and some nondecomposable things are not permitted to be interred with the remains, enabling natural decay and incorporation into the marine ecosystem.

Addressing environmental considerations is crucial in understanding the impact of burials at sea. Some may be concerned that sea burial activities damage marine habitats or constitute littering. However, funeral directors (such as McKenzie of McKenzie Mortuary Services in Long Beach) argue otherwise (Pineda, 2023). They highlight the natural process of putrefaction, in which the body gradually decomposes, releasing nutrients into the ocean and contributing to the ecosystem. McKenzie emphasizes that burials at sea are akin to artificial reef creation, benefiting marine life in the long term.

Exploring the Traditions of Burial at Sea

For Civilians

When arranging a burial at sea with a private company, families have considerable control over the ceremony's proceedings (Johnson, 2022). Usually, the package includes an hour of total time, with 30 minutes reserved for the ceremony at sea. Additional time can be arranged through upgrades, usually in 30-minute increments.

Customization and Personalization

Families can personalize the ceremony to match the wishes and personality of their loved ones. This could include a speech or message presented by a member of the church or family as a brief homage to the deceased. Attendees may also have the opportunity to share special memories or tributes during a designated time for sharing.

Musical Tributes and Video Presentations

Special music can be used at the ceremony, either live or via the boat's intercom system. Families often select meaningful tunes or invite a musician to play. Furthermore, families can choose to display a video tribute in the cabin before the committal, providing a visual reminder of their loved one's life.

Committing the Body to the Sea

During the ceremony, the captain and a crew member will respectfully commit the body to the sea, saying their final farewell. This moment is deeply meaningful to guests because it represents their loved one's spirit entering the wide expanse of the ocean.

Symbolic Gestures

Optional symbolic gestures, such as laying a wreath or dropping rose petals on the water's surface, can add a moving touch to the ceremony. These acts of remembrance serve to honor the memory of the departed while also providing consolation to bereaved family and friends.

Final Words and Prayers

The ceremony typically closes with a final speech or prayer from a family member or cleric. This moment of reflection allows attendees to express their love and gratitude for the deceased's life while also seeking solace in shared memories.

For Military Veterans

Burials at sea conducted by the Navy follow a distinct protocol, honoring the service and sacrifice of military veterans. However, it's important to note that these ceremonies take place when the ship is deployed, so family and friends cannot attend.

Military Protocol

The firing squad, casket bearers, and bugler are stationed first during the ritual. The ship's colors are lowered to half-mast, and the crew is assembled and called to attention.

Scripture and Prayer

A chaplain reads scripture, and attendees bow in humility while a prayer is spoken for the departed and their families. The body is then lowered into the water, accompanied by a gun salute and the playing of "Taps" by a bugler.

Presentation of the Flag

The flag is folded and given to the commanding officer, who can return it to the family along with a letter explaining the committal ceremony.

Honoring a Life Well Lived

Whether performed by a commercial firm or the military, burial at sea service is a respectable and meaningful way to say goodbye to a loved one. Attendees respect the memories of the fallen with unique tributes, symbolic gestures, and solemn rituals while finding comfort in the embrace of the ocean.

Reasons for Choosing Burial at Sea

Environmental Benefits and Considerations

Burial at sea offers several environmental benefits that appeal to individuals seeking a more eco-friendly end-of-life option. For starters, it permits the body to disintegrate organically in the ocean, which provides essential nutrients to marine life. This process reflects the natural cycle of life, as the body eventually integrates into the marine ecosystem. Unlike traditional burials, which use embalming chemicals and nonbiodegradable caskets, burial at sea has a low environmental impact and encourages sustainability.

Additionally, burials at sea can help ease the strain on land resources. Traditional cemeteries require vast amounts of land, which can contribute to urban sprawl and habitat loss. Individuals who choose burial at sea can help to save land and natural habitats, thus improving the long-term health of the environment.

Financial Considerations Compared to Traditional Burials

Financial considerations are also important in deciding whether to have a marine burial. Traditional burials can be prohibitively expensive, with costs for the purchase of caskets, burial plots, headstones, and maintenance fees. In comparison, burial at sea is often less expensive. While there may be fees for getting permits and planning the service, they are usually less than the costs connected with traditional funerals. This financial consideration can make burial at sea a more accessible choice for individuals and families looking for a respectful yet cost-effective end-of-life solution.

Personal Connection to the Ocean

For many people, the ocean holds a deep personal value. Whether through a lifelong love of sailing, fond memories of beach vacations, or a deep spiritual link to the sea, individuals may feel drawn to the idea of being buried in the vast expanse of the ocean. Burial at sea provides a means for people to honor their connection to the sea in a meaningful and symbolic way.

Furthermore, some people may have very personal reasons for choosing burial at sea. Perhaps they find comfort in the concept of eternal rest beneath the waves, or they yearn to be reunited with loved ones who have died before them. Whatever the reason, burial at sea allows people to express their unique desires and beliefs about the hereafter, bringing solace and closure to both themselves and their loved ones.

Maritime Tributes

Burial at sea is not a new concept; it has been a part of human history for ages. During times of conflict or scarcity (such as the Winter of Discontent described by Liverpool's medical officer of health Duncan Dolton in the 1970s), burial at sea emerged as an acceptable option (SwanSong Burial at Sea, 2018). Over the years, it has evolved into a ceremonial tribute to those who have dedicated their lives to the sea or who simply have a strong affinity with it.

One of the most famous figures to be buried at sea is Francis Drake, the legendary mariner known for his exploits during the Elizabethan era. Upon his death in 1596, Drake was buried in full armor and sealed in a lead coffin to keep his adversaries (mainly the Spanish) from discovering his remains. Despite several attempts to find his remains, Drake's final resting place remains unknown to this day.

In recent years, celebrities such as Robin Williams have chosen burial at sea as a means to say goodbye to the world. The renowned actor noted for his contagious wit and emotional performances, was laid to rest in the San Francisco Bay in 2014. Williams' decision to be buried at sea reflects his deep love for nature and his desire to return to the elements that brought him solace throughout his life.

Similarly, the ashes of John F. Kennedy Jr., the son of the ex-President of the United States, John F. Kennedy, were scattered at sea together with those of his wife Carolyn Bessette and her sister Lauren, following their terrible plane accident in 1999. JFK Jr., as a member of the renowned Kennedy family, represented hope and promise for many people, and his tragic death sent shockwaves around the world. His ultimate resting spot off the coast of Martha's Vineyard is a moving reflection of a life cut short.

H.G. Wells, a prolific author recognized for his innovative works of science fiction, was also buried at sea. His ashes were thrown near Old Harry Rocks, off the coast of Southern England, as a fitting homage to a man whose imagination was limitless. Wells' legacy has inspired generations of readers and authors, reminding us of the power of storytelling to extend beyond time and space.

Sir Edmund Hillary, the legendary mountaineer who scaled Everest, chose to have his ashes dispersed in Auckland's Hauraki Gulf after he died in 2008. Hillary's trek to the summit of Mount Everest demonstrated human resilience and determination, and his commitment to assisting Nepalese people through the Himalayan Trust is a legacy that lives on to this day.

In honoring these legends of the sea, we pay tribute not just to their astounding achievements but also to the eternal bond between humanity and the ocean. Burial at sea represents a return to the elements from where life begins, reminding us of our interdependence with the natural world. As we bid farewell to these famous personalities, may their spirits find peace in the vast expanse of the sea, where everyone is equal in the embrace of eternity.

Overall, as we reflect on the practice of burial at sea, it becomes evident that this method of burial holds profound implications for both individuals and the ecosystem. Beyond its ceremonial significance, sea burial provides a sustainable and environmentally favorable alternative to traditional burial practices. Returning the remains to the water helps to regenerate marine life and preserves our planet's delicate environment. Furthermore, the tradition allows people to express their deep connection to the ocean, commemorating their love of the sea in their final moments.

While burial at sea remains a timeless tradition, technological developments and environmental consciousness have resulted in the emergence of innovative burial methods. One such method is promession, also known as ice burial, which offers a sustainable approach to honoring the deceased while reducing environmental impact. The next chapter explores the concept of promession and its potential implications for the future of burial practices.

Chapter 10:

The Future - Ice Burial (Promession)

Step into a realm where science meets reverence, and tradition intertwines with innovation. In this chapter, we explore the future of body disposition methods, as guided by the allure of promession. Developed by Swedish biologist Susanne Wiigh-Mäsak, the method offers a novel approach to bidding farewell to our loved ones, using freeze-drying technology to transform bodies into ethereal powder, marking a dramatic shift in our relationship with death and the environment.

The Allure of Futuristic Body Disposition Methods

As humanity progresses into the future, our perspectives on various aspects of life (including death) continue to evolve. While traditional burial and cremation have long been considered the norm, there is a growing interest in future options that combine innovation and environmental sustainability. Imagine leaving this world in a way that not only honors your wishes but also contributes positively to the planet's well-being. This allure motivates many people to investigate novel methods of body disposition that deviate from conventional practices.

Introducing Promession: A Novel Approach to Body Reduction

Among these innovative methods, promession stands out as a pioneering approach to how we bid farewell to our deceased. This method, developed in the late 1990s by Swedish biologist Susanne Wiigh-Mäsak, combines research and appreciation for nature (McNally, 2012). Unlike traditional cremation (which uses energy and releases carbon dioxide) and burial (which requires land and resources), promession offers a sustainable solution through freeze-drying technology.

Promession, pronounced "pro-mesh-shun," is the process of reducing a body to powder through a meticulously engineered process. But it's not just the end result that's revolutionary; it's the entire process through which the body undergoes this change. Consider an experience where scientific advancements respect the sanctity of life, and where technological innovation works in collaboration with environmental sustainability.

Susanne Wiigh-Mäsak's vision for promession was not merely to introduce a new technique of body disposition but to redefine our relationship with death itself. Despite her company's insolvency in 2015, Wiigh-Mäsak remained committed to promession until her death in September 2020. Her legacy is carried on by the ambassadors and representatives she trained; they continue to raise awareness and comprehension of this innovative approach.

However, promession is more than just a technique of body disposition; it reflects our changing relationship with death and the environment. Its legal acceptance in Sweden, the U.K., and South Korea speaks volumes about society's willingness to embrace innovation while preserving tradition.

In the pages that follow, we delve deeper into understanding the promession process, exploring its implications, legal status, and cultural significance. Join us on this journey through the future of body disposition, where ice becomes a vessel for transformation and burial evolves into a celebration of life and nature inexorably connected.

Development by Swedish Biologist Susanne Wiigh-Mäsak

Wiigh-Mäsak created promession as an environmentally beneficial alternative to standard burial and cremation processes. Drawing inspiration from nature's own decomposition processes, she devised a method for gently returning the human body to the ground while minimizing environmental damage.

This remarkable Swedish scientist's background in biology, combined with her strong awareness of life's interconnectivity, helped her embark on this groundbreaking endeavor. She realized the need for a process that was consistent with ecological principles while also offering a sense of reverence and closure for the deceased and their families. She worked tirelessly to bring her vision to life, sparking a new era in the field of body disposition.

Liquidation of Promessa Company in 2015

Despite Wiigh-Mäsak's pioneering efforts, promession faced its share of obstacles. Promessa Organic AB, the firm she formed to implement her ambition, ran into financial difficulties in 2015 and was eventually liquidated (Green Burial Council, n.d.-b). This setback marked a pivotal moment in the history of promession, casting uncertainty over its future and leaving many supporters disheartened.

The liquidation of Promessa Organic AB was a sobering reminder of the complexities involved in introducing disruptive innovations to established industries. It emphasized the importance of ongoing financial and institutional support when navigating the complexities of bringing an innovative product to market. However, as the company struggled, Wiigh-Mäsak's enthusiasm for promession remained strong, serving as a beacon of hope for its eventual revival.

Wiigh-Mäsak's Legacy and Dedication to Promession

Despite the difficulties she encountered, Wiigh-Mäsak's commitment to promession never wavered. Even after Promessa Organic AB was liquidated, she remained committed to her mission by training Promessa representatives and ambassadors. Her tireless efforts helped to keep the flame of promession alive, inspiring a new generation of advocates who shared her goal for a more sustainable approach to body disposition.

Wiigh-Mäsak's legacy extends far beyond her contributions to science and technology, as evidenced by promession's long-lasting impact on the field of body disposition. Her unrelenting commitment to environmental sustainability, as well as her vision for a more compassionate approach to death, have had a lasting impact on society. Though she tragically succumbed to cancer in September 2020, her spirit lives on in the hearts and minds of people who continue to champion the ideals she believed in.

The Promession Process Unveiled

Promession stands out among futuristic body disposition procedures as an innovative solution, providing a unique and environmentally beneficial alternative to traditional burials and cremations. Let's delve deeper into the intricate steps involved in the promession process

(Fortino, 2021), revealing its science fiction-like complexities and practical applications.

Cryogenic Freezing Chamber Initiation

Imagine stepping into a chamber that feels like a gateway to the future, where the boundary between science and science fiction blurs. The promession process begins as the deceased is gently placed into a cryogenic freezing chamber, which resembles something out of a futuristic sci-fi film. This chamber serves as the starting point for the upcoming transformational process.

Liquid Nitrogen Application and Crystallization of Body Cells

Once inside the freezing chamber, the body is met with a frigid blast of liquid nitrogen, a substance colder than Antarctica's darkest winters. This severe cold, which can reach -196 degrees Celsius (-320.8 degrees Fahrenheit), causes the body's cells to freeze in a rapid and controlled way. The once-living tissues gradually turn into crystalline structures like delicate ice sculptures, preserving the essence of the deceased.

Mechanically Induced Vibration for Cell Disintegration

As the body solidifies in the freezing chamber, the next stage of this process begins with a mesmerizing display of mechanical precision. Vibrations, meticulously calibrated and controlled, reverberate within the chamber, causing the frozen cells to disintegrate. It's as if the very essence of the individual is being liberated from its physical form, ready to embark on its next adventure.

Sublimation

The body is now fragmented into countless microscopic particles, setting the stage for one of the most intriguing aspects of promession: sublimation. This process, similar to alchemy, involves the direct transformation of solid matter into vapor without first passing through a liquid phase. Within a vacuum chamber, the frozen particles undergo a miraculous transformation, transcending their physical form and soaring into the ethereal realm of vapor.

Resulting Powder

As the sublimation process concludes, what remains is a fine, powdery substance—only a fraction of the deceased's original weight. This powder, which contains the essence of many memories and experiences, represents the culmination of the promession process. It is both a tangible remnant and a symbol of transition, capturing the spirit of transformation and renewal.

Overall, the promession process unfolds as a captivating blend of science and imagination, providing a glimpse into a future in which traditional conceptions of death and burial are reinterpreted. From the initiation within the cryogenic freezing chamber to the final transformation into a delicate powder, each step in the promession experience demonstrates the ingenuity of human innovation and the endless possibilities of the future.

Handling and Preparation of Remains

Removal of Metals Through Magnetic or Sieving Processes

One of the key steps in the promession process is to carefully extract any metals found in the deceased individual's remains. This is a crucial aspect as it ensures that the final powder obtained is free of any metallic elements that could contaminate the environment when dispersed.

To achieve this, advanced techniques employing magnets or sieves are employed. Metals like dental fillings, surgical implants, and other metallic objects in the body are identified and removed from the powdery remains. This careful process ensures the purity of the end product, which is crucial for both environmental sustainability and the integrity of the promession method. This attention to detail further demonstrates promession practitioners' dedication to upholding the highest possible standards of environmental stewardship and respect for the deceased.

Containment in Biodegradable Materials

Following the completion of the final disposition process and the removal of metals, the resulting powder (which accounts for roughly 30% of the deceased person's original weight) is carefully enclosed within biodegradable materials. This phase is vital not only for the respectful treatment of the remains but also for the reduction of the environmental impact of the final disposition.

Biodegradable containers, usually made of plant fibers or recycled paper, are chosen for their ability to break down naturally over time. By using such materials, promession practitioners ensure that the burial of the remains does not contribute to long-term environmental degradation.

Furthermore, the use of biodegradable containers aligns with the principles of sustainability and ecological consciousness, demonstrating a holistic approach to end-of-life practices. Through the selection of environmentally friendly materials for containment, promession advocates display a deep-seated commitment to decreasing the ecological footprint associated with traditional burial practices.

Ethical and Environmental Considerations

The adoption of promession as a viable alternative to traditional burial procedures necessitates a rethinking of both ethical and environmental concerns in end-of-life care. Ethically, this strategy allows individuals to select a disposition that is consistent with their beliefs and values.

Furthermore, promession's environmentally responsible method addresses growing concerns about the environmental impact of traditional burial procedures, such as land utilization and the use of nonbiodegradable materials. Promession reduces environmental impact by using freeze-drying technology and biodegradable containers, allowing for natural disintegration.

By adopting such creative techniques, society can promote a more sustainable and ethical approach to death care, leaving a legacy of responsible stewardship for future generations.

Legal and Cultural Acceptance

Current Legal Status in Sweden, the U.K., and South Korea

Promession, with its novel approach to body disposition, has progressively achieved legal approval in a few nations, including Sweden, the United Kingdom, and

South Korea (Fortino, 2021). Each country has addressed the legalization of promession with a distinct set of rules and considerations.

- **Sweden:** As the birthplace of promession and its founder Susanne Wiigh-Mäsak, the nation is unsurprising in its embrace of this alternative to traditional burial and cremation methods (Zyga, 2011). The Swedish legal system recognizes promession as a viable option for anyone looking for environmentally friendly and space-saving burial solutions. The approach is consistent with Sweden's dedication to sustainability and innovation, making it a natural fit within the country's legal framework.

- **The U.K.:** Promession has found a place in the legal landscape, albeit with certain regulatory challenges to surmount. While not as popular as cremation or burial, promession has been regarded as a legitimate option for body disposition. The UK government established standards and regulations to ensure the safe and ethical use of promession, including requirements for licensing and oversight of facilities offering the service.

- **South Korea:** A country noted for its forward-thinking dedication to technology and innovation, South Korea has also adopted promession as an alternative to traditional burial techniques. The South Korean government has recognized this final disposition method's environmental benefits, especially in highly populated urban regions with little room for traditional cemeteries. Legal frameworks have been built to control this practice and ensure that human remains are handled and disposed of properly.

Despite the legal acceptance of promession in these countries, challenges remain in terms of widespread adoption and accessibility. Facilities that provide promession services are still few, and public awareness might be inadequate. However, as demand for eco-friendly and sustainable burial options continues to increase, the legal status of promession is likely to evolve to accommodate increased demand and interest.

Societal Perceptions and Cultural Implications

Acceptance of promession extends beyond legal structures to include societal and cultural attitudes on death and body disposition. While some people support promession as a progressive and environmentally conscientious decision, others may be skeptical or hesitant owing to cultural and religious views.

- **Environmental consciousness:** One of the primary drivers behind the acceptance of promession is its environmental friendliness. Promession appeals to people who value sustainability and eco-consciousness since it minimizes resource consumption and reduces carbon emissions connected with traditional burial and cremation. For these individuals, promession represents a way to leave a smaller ecological footprint even in death.

- **Cultural and religious considerations:** Despite its environmental benefits, promession may face opposition from cultural and religious groups who follow traditional burial customs or hold certain beliefs regarding the handling of human remains. It can be viewed with skepticism or rejection in societies where burial practices are very meaningful and cremation is considered forbidden. Proponents of promession need to engage with these communities respectfully and address concerns about cultural sensitivity and religious beliefs.

- **Changing attitudes:** Urbanization, environmental awareness, and technological advancements have all contributed to a shift in society's attitudes on death and body disposition. As younger generations seek alternatives to traditional burial methods and promote sustainability, promession may become more widely accepted and normalized. Open dialogue and education about the benefits and procedures of promession can help develop positive perceptions and increase cultural acceptance over time.

Ultimately, while promession has both legal and cultural hurdles, its unique approach to body disposition shows promise as a sustainable and environmentally friendly alternative to traditional burial and cremation. By navigating regulatory frameworks, resolving cultural sensitivities, and promoting awareness, promession advocates can fight to increase the acceptance and accessibility of this innovative technology.

Reflecting on the Potential of Promession

Promession, with its novel approach to body disposition, opens the door to a future in which death is treated with reverence and sustainability (Grundhauser, 2016). The approach challenges established procedures by providing a process that not only reduces the body to powder but also has a low environmental impact. When considering its potential, one can't help but imagine a society in which death is not just a natural transition, but also a means of positively impacting the environment.

The technique's ability to decrease the deceased to a fraction of their former weight offers various benefits. For starters, it provides a dignified method of dealing with human remains, letting loved ones say their goodbyes while respecting both the individual and the environment. Additionally, its eco-friendly nature addresses concerns about the environmental impact of traditional burial and cremation practices. By combining freeze-drying technology and biodegradable materials, promession reduces pollution and land use associated with conventional funeral practices.

Moreover, promession represents a shift in cultural attitudes toward death and the afterlife. As societies become more environmentally conscious, there is an increasing demand for end-of-life practices that are consistent with ecological ideals. Promession not only meets this need, but also promotes a more in-depth discussion on mortality, sustainability, and our interconnectedness with the natural world.

Future of Body Disposition Technology

The future of promession, and body disposition technology in general, is extremely promising. As people become more aware of environmental issues, there will be a greater demand for environmentally friendly funeral practices. Promession, with its eco-friendly strategy and low carbon footprint, is poised to gain traction not only in its current legal jurisdictions but also globally.

In the coming years, research and development efforts may result in increased efficiency, cost-effectiveness, and overall product quality. This could involve advancements in cryogenic freezing, sublimation technology, and metal removal methods.

Furthermore, greater acceptability and legalization of promession in other nations could pave the way for widespread adoption. As more individuals and communities embrace this alternative method of body disposition, societal norms and cultural views regarding death and funeral rituals may evolve accordingly.

Looking ahead, promession's integration with other developing technologies has the potential to change the funeral industry. Consider personalized memorial services that include virtual reality, augmented reality, and biodegradable 3D-printed urns storing promession remains. These developments have the potential to provide a very individualized and ecologically sensitive method of honoring the departed.

In conclusion, promession represents not only a creative solution for the practical issues of body disposition but also a conceptual change toward a more sustainable and comprehensive approach to death and mourning. As we navigate the complexities of the modern world, promession serves as a beacon of innovation, reminding us that even in death, there is potential for growth, transformation, and rejuvenation.

Conclusion

In concluding *The Final Farewell: Exploring Post-Death Treatment Options*, I find myself overwhelmed with a profound sense of awe at the vast tapestry of human traditions and scientific discoveries that regulate our journey beyond death. Through the lens of this exploration, I've come to understand that our mortality is more than simply a statistical inevitability; it's a fundamentally human experience distinguished by cultural nuances, personal beliefs, and a search for meaning that goes beyond the physical domain.

One undeniable truth underscores all our lives: 100% mortality rate. No matter our wealth, status, or achievements, death is the great equalizer that unites us all. Yet, within this shared fate exists a wide range of options for what happens to our bodies once we depart from this world.

In the chapter on burial, we discovered the intricate web of cultural rituals and traditions that surround this ancient technique of body disposition. Whether it's done as an elaborate ceremony or a simple graveside gathering, burial serves as a profound reminder of our interconnectedness with the land and the cycle of life and death.

Then there's cremation, a practice that has gained popularity for its simplicity and versatility. From scattering ashes in meaningful locations to transforming them into keepsakes, cremation provides a variety of options for honoring the deceased while acknowledging the impermanence of life.

Whole-body donation to science emerges as a noble choice, allowing individuals to contribute to medical advancement and education even after death. It's a selfless deed that exemplifies the ethos of giving back to society and leaving a lasting legacy for future generations.

Let us not overlook the emerging trend of green or natural burial, which emphasizes sustainability and environmental awareness. By returning to the earth in a biodegradable manner, we not only reduce our ecological impact but also reinforce our connection to the natural world.

Aquamation, a modern alternative to traditional cremation, is a gentle process of alkaline hydrolysis that restores the body to its natural state. This practice protects the environment and provides families with a unique way to commemorate their loved ones.

Tree pod burial, another innovative approach, allows individuals to literally return to the land, stimulating the birth of new life as their remains contribute to the flourishing of trees. It represents a harmonious cycle of life and death, which connects us closely to nature.

Terramation, often known as human composting, is a novel concept in which our bodies naturally decompose to replenish the soil. This sustainable choice provides a meaningful connection to the Earth, encouraging rejuvenation and growth beyond our own lives.

Burial at sea, a time-honored tradition in many cultures, offers a serene and majestic farewell as our bodies return to the vastness of the ocean. It evokes a sense of freedom and eternal movement, respecting our relationship to the elements and the cycles of life.

Looking toward the future, ice burial (or promession) presents an intriguing approach for freeze-drying the body and transforming it into organic matter. This innovative approach reflects humanity's ongoing quest for sustainable and meaningful ways to honor the deceased.

Beyond the specifics of each method lies a deeper truth: our relationship with death is as diverse and intricate as life itself. Whether we select a traditional burial, a green choice, or future technologies, what counts most is the love, memories, and impact we leave behind. Our legacy isn't defined by the method of our departure but by the lives we've touched and the imprint we've left on the world.

This book has been a labor of love for me, motivated by a desire to demystify the subject of death and dying and spark meaningful conversations about it. I feel that understanding and following our loved ones' desires for their post-death arrangements allows us to honor them in the best possible way. If reading *The Final Farewell* has prompted you to reflect on your own wishes or to engage in conversations with your family and friends, I consider it a success.

I sincerely hope that you, the reader, have found value and insight within these pages. If this book has influenced your perspective or prompted thoughtful consideration, I would appreciate it if you would leave a review. Your candid feedback helps other readers discover the book's insights and merits, and I am eager to share this opportunity with a wider audience.

Thank you for participating in this adventure with me. May it inspire us all to embrace the wide range of possibilities for our final farewell, and to live each day with purpose, love, and gratitude.

What Can Be Done With the Ashes?

Unique Memorialization Ideas for Ashes

Custom Urns

Custom urns are a highly personal and meaningful way to honor a deceased loved one. These specialized containers go beyond conventional designs, allowing individuals or families to create a tribute that captures their deceased family member or friend's distinct personality.

However, finding the right artisan or company to craft a custom urn requires careful consideration. Families may wish to look into artists or businesses that specialize in this niche area. It is important to select someone who recognizes the significance of the tribute and can turn the dead individual's passions and personality into a tangible object. Factors to consider include craftsmanship, materials used, cost, and ability to satisfy specific requirements or designs.

For motorcycle enthusiasts or anyone with a passion for a particular hobby or interest, custom urns offer the opportunity to celebrate that aspect of their life in a meaningful way. Imagine a beautifully crafted urn shaped like the iconic gas tank of a Harley-Davidson motorcycle, complete with detailed decorations and personal touches. Such a tribute not only serves as a final resting place but also captures the individual's spirit and excitement, keeping their memory alive in a real and symbolic way.

In today's digital age, online platforms make it simple and accessible to explore custom urn possibilities. Family members can browse several websites specializing in memorial products and interact with artisans and designers from all over the world. These platforms often include portfolios, testimonials, and personalization choices, allowing people to envision and design a personalized urn that really honors their loved one's memory. Furthermore, internet platforms may include resources such as design tools, customer assistance, and direction throughout the customization process, making it easier for families to navigate this deeply personal journey of memorialization.

Incorporating Ashes Into Creative Expressions

Artistic Tributes

Turning ashes into artistic tributes offers a deeply personal and tangible way to remember loved ones (Chauhan, 2024). Artists have developed novel methods for incorporating ashes into many types of artwork, such as paintings and sculptures. Ashes can be blended with paint or inserted directly into the medium, providing texture and depth to the artwork. This approach enables the development of really unique works of art that serve as poignant reminders of the departed person's life.

Similarly, sculptors can include ashes in their work by combining them with materials like clay, resin, or metal. This procedure not only produces physically appealing sculptures but also imbues them with great emotional value because the ashes become an integral part of the artwork's composition.

Cremains-infused tattoos provide another unique and very personal choice for people who want to retain a permanent homage to their loved ones. Tattoo artists can blend a small amount of ashes with tattoo ink, allowing people to incorporate the essence of their beloved into a design that is meaningful to them. These tattoos serve as enduring memorials, symbolizing the lasting bond between the individual and their departed loved one.

Memorial jewelry and blown glass creations offer extra ways to remember the deceased via artistic expression. Jewelry designers can encase ashes in pendants, rings, or other jewelry pieces, allowing people to keep the memories of their dead close to their hearts at all times. Blown glass artists can incorporate ashes into glass sculptures or decorations, resulting in stunning and ethereal works that capture the essence of the deceased person.

These creative expressions not only serve as tangible reminders of the dead person's life but also bring comfort and peace to those left behind. By infusing ashes into artworks and personal souvenirs, individuals can create lasting tributes that honor and celebrate the unique spirit of their loved ones.

Unconventional Celebrations of Life

When it comes to remembering a loved family member or friend, some people look for unconventional ways to do it. Here, we look at some unique ways to bid farewell and leave an indelible impression on those left behind.

Spectacular Farewells: Creating Vibrant Firework Displays With Ashes

Imagine a sky illuminated not just by bursts of color but also by the essence of cherished memories. Memorial fireworks are a breathtaking and unconventional way to honor the departed (Powell, 2022). By adding a portion of the cremated remains to the fireworks, families can orchestrate a spectacular display, symbolizing the vibrancy of their loved one's life. Each explosion becomes a poignant reminder of the joy, laughter, and moments shared, casting a radiant glow across the heavens and the hearts of all who witness it.

Futuristic Farewells: Sending Ashes Into Space as a Cosmic Tribute

For those with an adventurous spirit and a yearning for the stars, space burials represent the ultimate cosmic tribute. By entrusting a portion of their loved one's ashes to spaceflight companies specializing in celestial memorials, families can embark on a journey beyond the confines of Earth. Whether launched into orbit around the earth or sent on an interplanetary course into the expanse of space, these futuristic farewells provide a profound opportunity to honor the eternal connection between the departed and the cosmos. As the ashes travel across space, they become part of the cosmic tapestry, incorporating their legacy into the fabric of the universe itself.

Environmental Consciousness: Transforming Ashes Into Artificial Coral Reefs

In an era where environmental sustainability is crucial, some people choose a memorial option that not only respects their loved one's memory but also helps to preserve marine ecosystems (Banks, 2020). By transforming ashes into artificial coral reefs, families can construct long-lasting sanctuaries teeming with life beneath the waters. These environmentally friendly memorials provide important habitats for aquatic species while also paying honor to the deceased. As the coral reef grows and thrives, it becomes a living witness to the enduring heritage of love and stewardship, resonating down the ocean's depths for future generations.

These unconventional celebrations of life provide poignant and meaningful ways to remember the departed, capturing the essence of their spirit and leaving an everlasting mark on those they leave behind.

About the Author

Bridget Marie is a woman who has had a multipath career. All paths were a great fit, and now, she has entered the indie publishing arena. With a passion for storytelling and a commitment to lifelong learning, Bridget is dedicated to creating captivating narratives for numerous books. Inspired by her deep love for her grandchildren, she has authored a trilogy of preschool activity books for children, along with a collection of coloring books. Any time they color or learn together with the preschool books is such a joyful time.

When Bridget is not writing, she enjoys lunch dates with her husband, visits with her grown children and grandchildren, and indulges in playtime with her standard poodles, game nights with her friends, or any kind of organizing. Her writing style is just like her life—casual and comfy. She will inform where she can, but will always follow her heart to things that bring her—and, hopefully, you—joy.

References

7 embalming alternatives: Lower cost for higher meaning. (2023, December 22). Endly. https://endly.co/embalming-alternatives/

7 innovative burial alternatives: Beyond the usual grave. (n.d.). Better Place Forests. Retrieved March 2, 2024, from https://www.betterplaceforests.com/blog/7-innovative-burial-alternatives/

All about aquamation: Cremation alternatives for humans and pets. (n.d.). Better Place Forests. Retrieved March 2, 2024, from https://www.betterplaceforests.com/blog/all-about-aquamation-cremation-alternatives-for-humans-and-pets/

Alterna Cremation. (2024, January 12). *Cremation myths debunked: Separating fact from fiction.* https://alternacremation.ca/blogs/blog-entries/2/Blog/80/Cremation-Myths-Debunked-Separating-Fact-From-Fiction.html

American Heritage. (2021, November 5). *Why you should choose burial.* https://blog.thehealingstartshere.com/2021/11/why-you-should-choose-burial/

Arthur, G. (2023, June 23). *The rise of cremation and what it means for deathcare providers.* PlotBox. https://plotbox.com/blog/the-rise-of-cremation-and-what-it-means-for-deathcare-providers

AshestoAshes. (2024, March 17). *The eco-friendly advantages of cremation: A sustainable end-of-life option.* Ashes to Ashes Corporation. https://ashestoashesinc.com/eco-friendly-advantages-of-cremation/

Aura Flights. (2023, June 14). *Burial or cremation | What's right for you?* https://www.ashesinspace.co.uk/post/burial-or-cremation

Baldwin, A. (2022, November 23). *What is terramation?* Funeral Choice. https://www.yourfuneralchoice.com/planning-funeral/what-is-terramation/

Balta, J. Y., Venne, G., & Noël, G. P. J. C. (2022). *10 tips on working with human body donors in medical training and research.* Anatomical Science International, 97(3), 307–312. https://www.ncbi.nlm.nih.gov/pmc/articles/PMC9167808/

Banks, L. (2020, September 4). *Buried at sea – Resting in an artificial coral reef.* OneWorld Memorials. https://www.oneworldmemorials.com/blogs/news/18465347-resting-in-an-artificial-coral-reef

Barrett, C. (2019, July 31). *Biodegradable burial containers for green burial: Coffins & caskets*. Carolina Memorial Sanctuary. https://carolinamemorialsanctuary.org/biodegradable-burial-containers-for-green-burial-coffins-caskets/

The benefits of choosing a sea burial service for your loved one. (n.d.). Beyond the Sea. Retrieved March 3, 2024, from https://burialsinthesea.com/the-benefits-of-choosing-a-sea-burial-service-for-your-loved-one/

Benson, E. (2021, April 16). *Aquamation: The gentler alternative.* Paws into Grace. https://pawsintograce.com/aquamation-the-gentler-alternative/

Body composting. (n.d.). The Natural Funeral. Retrieved March 3, 2024, from https://www.thenaturalfuneral.com/natural-organic-reduction-body-composting/

Booth, S. (2018, September 23). *What happens to your body when it's donated to science?* Healthline. https://www.healthline.com/health-news/what-happens-to-your-body-when-its-donated-to-science

Brouillette, M. (2022, June 23). *Considering donating your body to science? Read this first.* Popular Mechanics. https://www.popularmechanics.com/science/health/a40393548/how-to-donate-your-body-to-science/

Caregiving.com. (2023, October 16). *Open communication during the end-of-life journey - Connecting with friends and family.* https://www.caregiving.com/osts/open-communication-during-the-end-of-life-journey-connecting-with-friends-and-family

Certified Safety Training. (2023, November 3). *The formaldehyde standard for funeral professionals.* https://certifiedsafetytraining.org/blogs/news/the-formaldehyde-standard-for-funeral-professionals

Chauhan, A. (2024, March 14). *10 creative things to do with cremated remains.* Eirene. https://eirenecremations.com/blog/10-creative-things-to-do-with-cremated-remains

christy.kessler. (2020, February 5). *What you need to know about burial at sea.* Funeral Basics. https://www.funeralbasics.org/need-know-about-burial-sea/

Coffins, shrouds and urns. (n.d.). Leedam Natural Burials. Retrieved March 12, 2024, from https://www.leedam.com/advice/coffins-shrouds-and-urns/

Colorado Palliative & Hospice Care. (2023, September 27). *Navigating end-of-life discussions with family.* https://www.coloradophc.com/navigating-end-of-life-discussions-with-family/

Cultural and religious perspectives on cremation. (2023, May 22). Mangano Family Funeral Homes, Inc.

https://www.manganofh.com/cultural-and-religious-perspectives-on-cremation

Day, N. (2022, November 25). *Is DNA testing possible after cremation?* Trupoint Memorials. https://trupointmemorials.com/a/s/answers/cremation/is-dna-testing-possible-after-cremation

Dermond, J. (2024, February 28). *Human composting: A new future for our dead?* NU Sci Magazine. https://nuscimagazine.com/human-composting-a-new-future-for-our-dead/

Donate my body to science. (n.d.). United Tissue Network. Retrieved March 2, 2024, from https://unitedtissue.org/donate-my-body-to-science/

Donate your body to science. (2009). Physicians Committee for Responsible Medicine. https://www.pcrm.org/ethical-science/animal-testing-and-alternatives/donate-your-body-to-science

Donation. (n.d.). NJSFDA. Retrieved March 5, 2024, from https://web.njsfda.org/public/consumer/funeral-planning-options/disposition-options/donation

Elliott, J. K. (2019, June 2). *A green death: Is human composting or natural burial for you?* Global News. https://globalnews.ca/news/5329686/human-composting-green-burial/

The embalming process (Explicit). (2019). Everplans. https://www.everplans.com/articles/the-embalming-process-explicit

Engage Team. (2016, October 24). *How is a body cremated?* Hutchison Funeral Home. https://www.hutchisonfuneralhome.com/how-is-a-body-cremated

EPA. (2012). *5.2 dissolved oxygen and biochemical oxygen demand.* https://archive.epa.gov/water/archive/web/html/vms52.html

Eterneva. (n.d.). *What is aquamation and what is left after?* Retrieved March 5, 2024, from https://www.eterneva.com/resources/aquamation-process

Ever Loved. (2020, October 10). *6 reasons to pre-plan your funeral.* FreeWill. https://www.freewill.com/learn/6-reasons-to-pre-plan-your-funeral

Ever Loved. (2023, December 18). *What is the mushroom burial suit?* https://everloved.com/articles/funeral-planning/what-is-the-mushroom-burial-suit/

Ever Loved. (2024, January 21). *What is a tree pod burial?* https://everloved.com/articles/funeral-planning/what-is-a-tree-pod-burial/

Exploring the process of burial at sea - About burial at sea. (2023b, July 20). Return Home.

https://returnhome.com/exploring-the-process-of-burial-at-sea/

Formaldehyde and cancer risk. (2022, October 24). American Cancer Society. https://www.cancer.org/cancer/risk-prevention/chemicals/formaldehyde.html

Fortino, D. (2021, September 24). *What is promession? A guide to a new funerary process.* Eirene. https://eirenecremations.com/blog/what-is-promession

Fortino, D. (2022, October 19). *What the major religions say about cremation.* Eirene. https://eirenecremations.com/blog/major-religions-cremation

Fortino, D. (2023, April 19). *What is "aquamation"? A sustainable cremation alternative called alkaline hydrolysis.* Eirene. https://eirenecremations.com/blog/understanding-aquamation

Fortino, D. (2024, February 8). *How the mushroom burial suit works and what does it cost.* Eirene. https://eirenecremations.com/blog/how-mushroom-burial-suit-works

Frequently asked questions (FAQs). (n.d.). University of Michigan - Michigan Medicine. Retrieved March, 1, 2024, from https://medicine.umich.edu/dept/anatomical-sciences/anatomical-donations-program/frequently-asked-questions-faqs

Funnell, A. (2018, June 28). *Freeze-drying, shattering, dissolving: Weird ways to dispose of a body (legally)*. ABC News. https://www.abc.net.au/news/2018-06-28/the-future-of-body-disposal/9894804

Global embalming chemicals market 2024-2030 | March 2024 updated. (n.d.). Mobility Foresights. Retrieved March 1, 2024, from https://mobilityforesights.com/product/embalming-chemicals-market/

Gonzales, M. (2021, February 6). *What is aquamation? Everything you need to know*. Green Cremation Texas. https://www.cremation.green/what-is-aquamation/

Green burial defined. (n.d.). Green Burial Council. Retrieved March 7, 2024, from https://www.greenburialcouncil.org/green_burial_defined.html

Grundhauser, E. (2016, February 25). *A burial machine that will freeze your corpse, vibrate it to dust, and turn it into soil*. Atlas Obscura. https://www.atlasobscura.com/articles/a-burial-machine-that-will-freeze-your-corpse-vibrate-it-to-dust-and-turn-it-into-soil

Guide to green burial – A natural approach to funerals. (n.d.). Lincoln Heritage Life Insurance Company. Retrieved March 12, 2024, from https://www.lhlic.com/consumer-resources/green-burial/

Harries, T. (2023, May 4). *Tree pod burial explained: Becoming a tree after death.* Earth. https://earthfuneral.com/resources/tree-pod-burial-explained/

Hoffner, A. (2018, May 24). *I haven't marked my father's grave.* Green Burial Naturally. https://www.greenburialnaturally.org/blog/tag/Grave+markers#:~:text=Green%20burial%20cemeteries%20choose%20to

Houser, K. (2022, September 30). *Human composting is now legal in five states.* Freethink. https://www.freethink.com/culture/human-composting

How to donate your body to science. (2023, August 15). Meri. https://www.meri.org/resource/news/how-to-donate-body-to-science/

Jacobson, D. I., & Madden, H. (2022, October 25). *How to be buried as a tree.* WikiHow. https://www.wikihow.com/Be-Buried-As-a-Tree

Johnson, S. (2022, April 22). *A guide to burials at sea for civilian & military burials.* Cake. https://www.joincake.com/blog/burial-at-sea-civilians-navy-guide/

Kaplan, D. (n.d.). *The complete guide to cremation (Updated).* Willed. Retrieved March 9, 2024, from https://www.willed.com.au/guides/cremation-australia/

Keeley, M. (2017). Family communication at the end of life. *Behavioral Sciences, (7)*3, p. 45. https://www.ncbi.nlm.nih.gov/pmc/articles/PMC5618053/

Keene, V. (2019, August 20). *Water cremation and aquamation laws in your state.* Nolo. https://www.nolo.com/legal-encyclopedia/alkaline-hydrolysis-laws-your-state.html

Kessler, S. (2022, April 22). *What's the process for a traditional burial? 10 steps explained.* Cake. https://www.joincake.com/blog/what-is-the-burial-process/

Key, E. (2022, September 14). *Continuing the life cycle with green burials.* The Sopris Sun. https://soprissun.com/continuing-the-life-cycle-with-green-burials/

Lamberg, E. (n.d.). *The pros and cons of burial.* USA TODAY. Retrieved March 10, 2024, from https://www.usatoday.com/story/community-hub/funeral-planning/2020/03/24/burial-pros-and-cons/5065254002/

Lang, D., Cone, N., Lally, M., Valentine-French, S., Carter, S., & Clark-Plaskie, M. (2022). *Emotions and attitudes related to death.* Iowa State University Digital Press. https://iastate.pressbooks.pub/individualfamilydevelopment/chapter/emotions-attitudes-related-to-death/

Markoe, L. (2014, January 23). *Green burials reflect a shift to care for the body and soul.* Religion News Service. https://religionnews.com/2014/01/23/green-burials-reflect-shift-care-body-soul/

Martin, A. (2024, March 21). *Tree pod burial: How it works + costs [2024].* Choice Mutual. https://choicemutual.com/blog/tree-pod-burial/

McDonald, M. (2023, January 21). *'Human composting' debate: A deeper dive into the Catholic teaching on the dignity of human remains.* National Catholic Register. https://www.ncregister.com/news/human-composting-debate-a-deeper-dive-into-the-catholic-teaching-on-the-dignity-of-human-remains

McGee, A. (2023, July 8). *Where is aquamation legal? Which states have legalized aquamation or bio cremation?* US Funerals Online. https://www.us-funerals.com/where-is-aquamation-legal-which-states-have-legalized-aquamation-or-bio-cremation/

McLean, M. (2016, September 28). *Answering your green burial questions.* https://www.funeralbasics.org/what-is-green-burial/

McNally, P. (2012, July 14). *Promession: A return to the living soil.* The Daily Undertaker. http://www.dailyundertaker.com/2008/09/promession-return-to-living-soil.html

MedCure. (2019, November 26). *Talking to your family about body donation.* https://medcure.org/talking-to-your-family-about-body-donation/

Mendoza, R. L. (2023, September 19). *Debunking cremation myths.* Golden Haven. https://www.goldenhaven.com.ph/blog/debunking-cremation-myths/

Milano, S. (2018, July 15). *Why did we start burying our deceased?* Locust Valley Cemetery. https://www.lvcemetery.com/why-bury.html

Milton Fields Georgia. (2019, December 31). *Why conventional burial harms the environment.* Milton Fields. https://miltonfieldsgeorgia.com/conventional-burial-harms-environment/

Mornington Green. (2022, June 28). *Cremation or burial: How to decide what option is right for you.* Mornington Green Legacy Gardens. https://morningtongreen.com.au/cremation-or-burial-how-to-decide-what-option-is-right-for-you/

Oster, L. (2022, July 27). *Could water cremation become the new American way of death?* Smithsonian Magazine. https://www.smithsonianmag.com/innovation/could-water-cremation-become-the-new-american-way-of-death-180980479/

Other disposition options. (n.d.). Green Burial Council. Retreived March 7, 2024, from

https://www.greenburialcouncil.org/other_disp
osition_options.html

Pineda, D. (2023, April 7). *Eternal slumber at sea.*
Beachcomber.
https://beachcomber.news/content/eternal-
slumber-sea

Pizza, A. (2023, February 23). *Human composting 101: How
terramation is bettering the planet.* Brightly.
https://brightly.eco/blog/human-composting

postlaunch. (2023, August 1). *The importance of end-of-life
planning.* Michaelson Law.
https://michaelsonlaw.com/the-importance-of-
end-of-life-planning/

Powell, C. (2022, March 31). *20+ ideas on what to do with
cremation ashes.* Pure Cremation.
https://purecremation.co.uk/blog/what-to-do-
with-ashes

Powell, C. (2023, July 24). *How is a body prepared for
cremation.* Pure Cremation.
https://purecremation.co.uk/blog/how-is-a-
body-prepared-for-cremation

Ramirez, D. (2023, November 2). *Burial at sea: How it
works and how to plan.* NerdWallet.
https://www.nerdwallet.com/article/investing/
estate-planning/burial-at-sea

Ray, D. (2024, February 4). *Simple guide to tree pod burial in
2024.* Pinnacle Quote.

https://www.pinnaclequote.com/blog/tree-pod-burial/

Raymond, C. (2024a, January 20). *What is promession and how does it work?* Funeral Help Center. https://www.funeralhelpcenter.com/what-is-promession-and-how-does-it-work/

Raymond, C. (2024b, March 12). *What is alkaline hydrolysis and how does it work?* Verywell Health. https://www.verywellhealth.com/what-is-alkaline-hydrolysis-1131908

The real environmental impact of funeral options, Part 1: Traditional burial. (2023, May 26). Death Curious. https://deathcurious.com/environmental-impact-of-traditional-burial/

Recompose — Our model. (n.d.). Recompose. Retrieved March 2, 2024, from https://recompose.life/our-model/

Research for Life. (2022, May 18). *Tree pod burials: A life after death.* https://researchforlife.org/blog/tree-pod-burials/

Schilling Funeral Home & Cremation. (2021, August 2). *The differences between caskets and coffins.* https://schillingfuneralhome.com/blogs/blog-entries/9/Blogs/115/The-Differences-Between-Caskets-and-Coffins.html

Shah, R. (2024, April 10). *Tree pod burial cost.* GetSure. https://getsure.org/tree-pod-burial-cost/

Shah, S. (2018, April 16). *Freeze-dried death that turns your body into powder could replace cremation, claims its creator.* The Sun. https://www.thesun.co.uk/tech/science/6065136/freeze-dried-death-promession-cremation-burial/

Shandilya, A. (2022, January 4). *What is aquamation cremation? Is it legal and how much does it cost? Details inside.* Republic. https://www.republicworld.com/world-news/what-is-aquamation-cremation-is-it-legal-and-how-much-does-it-cost-details-inside-articleshow/

Sieger, K. (2018, October 29). *Body donation - a gift with emotional hurdles.* Karin Sieger - Online Psychotherapy. https://karinsieger.com/body-donation-medical-training-research/

Spence, L. (2019, May 10). *The art of goodbye: Planning final arrangements.* University of Florida IFAS Extension. https://edis.ifas.ufl.edu/publication/FY1466

Stuart-Ulin, C. R. (2019, October 29). *Green burials: Everything you need to know about the growing trend.* CBC. https://www.cbc.ca/life/culture/green-burials-everything-you-need-to-know-about-the-growing-trend-1.5340000

SwanSong Burial at Sea. (2018, September 19). *Famous people buried at sea.* https://swansongburial.com/blog/famous-people-buried-at-sea/

Tack, T. (2017, August 1). *The embalming process.* Basic Funerals and Cremation Choices. https://www.basicfunerals.ca/funeral-industry/the-embalming-process

TalkDeath. (2018, January 22). *Burial at sea: Everything you need to know.* https://www.talkdeath.com/burial-at-sea-everything-need-to-know/

TalkDeath. (2021, April 27). *Five things you didn't know about water cremation.* https://www.talkdeath.com/five-things-you-didnt-know-about-water-cremation/

Tamplin, T. (2023, March 27). *Cremation.* Finance Strategists. https://www.financestrategists.com/financial-advisor/cremation/

Tan, S. (2021, August 31). *What are green burials?* WebMD. https://www.webmd.com/a-to-z-guides/features/what-are-green-burials

Team Earth. (2022, April 12). *What is terramation?* Earth Funeral Group. https://earthfuneral.com/resources/what-is-terramation/

Team Earth. (2023, February 2). *Tracker: Where is alkaline hydrolysis legal in the US?* Earth Funeral Group. https://earthfuneral.com/resources/tracker-where-alkaline-hydrolysis-legal/

Team Endly. (2023, November 24). *How long does a body last in a green burial: From womb to nature.* Endly.

https://endly.co/how-long-does-a-body-last-in-a-green-burial/

Tomorrow Bio. (2021, July 26). *Different societies' attitudes and rituals towards death.* https://www.tomorrow.bio/post/what-are-different-societies-attitudes-towards-death

Tree burial pods: A comprehensive guide. (2021, February 5). The Living Urn. https://www.thelivingurn.com/blogs/news/tree-burial-pods-a-comprehensive-guide

Tree burial pods: An eco-friendly alternative to traditional burials. (n.d.). Better Place Forests. Retrieved March 2, 2024, from https://www.betterplaceforests.com/blog/tree-burial-pods-an-eco-friendly-alternative-to-traditional-burials/

Trusted Caskets Admin. (2023). *How long does it take for a body to decompose in the casket.* Trusted Caskets. https://trustedcaskets.com/blogs/news/how-long-does-it-take-for-a-body-to-decompose-in-the-casket

Tufnell, N. (2013, October 14). *Freeze-drying the dead could help save the planet.* Wired. https://www.wired.com/story/promessa/

Turner, C. (2022, May 11). *Green burials: A greener alternative to traditional burial.* Green and Prosperous. https://www.greenandprosperous.com/blog/gr

een-burials-a-greener-alternative-to-traditional-burial

Understanding whole body donation. (n.d.). Research for life. March 14, 2024, from https://researchforlife.org/understanding-whole-body-donation/

United States Environmental Protection Agency. (2024, April 8). *Burial at sea.* https://www.epa.gov/ocean-dumping/burial-sea

UNOS. (n.d.). *Deceased donation.* Retrieved March 13, 2024, from https://unos.org/transplant/deceased-donation/

VanderVaate, R. (2024, April 3). *Tree pod burial & green burials 2024.* Funeral Funds of America. https://funeralfunds.com/tree-pod-burial-green-burials/

Varghese, A. M. (2022, January 12). *Explained: What is aquamation, the cremation method opted by Desmond Tutu?* The Week. https://www.theweek.in/news/sci-tech/2022/01/12/explained-what-is-aquamation-the-cremation-method-opted-by-desmond-tutu.html

Walas, M. (2015, September 21). *Biolife, LLC introduces the living urn for people.* The Living Urn. https://www.thelivingurn.com/blogs/news/45

047681-biolife-llc-introduces-the-living-urn-for-people

Walas, M. (2024, March 17). *25 unique memorial service ideas for 2024.* The Living Urn. https://www.thelivingurn.com/blogs/news/memorial-service-ideas

Wallace, T. (n.d.). *13 best cremation ashes ideas to memorialize your loved ones.* Eterneva. Retrieved March 5, 2024, from https://www.eterneva.com/resources/what-to-do-with-cremation-ashes

Weber, F. (2023, July 5). *Hinduism cremation.* Eulogy Assistant. https://eulogyassistant.com/hinduism-cremation/

Webster, L. (n.d.-a). *To lie down in green pastures: How the Catholic church is leading the way in green burial.* Green Burial Council. Retrieved March 3, 2024, from https://www.greenburialcouncil.org/the-catholic-church-and-green-burial.html

Webster, L. (n.d.-b). *Top 10 real answers to questions real people ask about green burial.* Green Burial Council. Retrieved March 3, 2024, from https://www.greenburialcouncil.org/real_answers_question_about_green_burial.htm

What are green and natural burials? (n.d.). A. B. Walker. Retrieved March 1, 2024, from https://www.abwalker.co.uk/arranging-a-

funeral/types-of-funerals/green-and-natural-
burial/

What is aquamation? The complete guide for veterinarians. (2022,
July 16). DaySmart Vet.
https://www.daysmart.com/vet/blog/what-is-
aquamation-the-complete-guide-for-
veterinarians/

What it means to be green. (n.d.). NFDA. Retrieved March
10, 2024, from
https://nfda.org/resources/business-
technical/green-funeral-practices/what-it-
means-to-be-green

Which one is ecologically the best option: Cremation or burial?
(2021, February 11). Heart in Diamond.
https://www.heart-in-
diamond.com/news/blogpost/burial-
cremation-eco-options.html

Why human composting could be the future of remains processing.
(2023a, January 7). Return Home.
https://returnhome.com/human-composting-
future-of-remains-processing/

Winemaker, S. (2021, August). *Five common misconceptions
about dying.* Hamilton Jewish News.
https://www.hamiltonjewishnews.com/home-
page/voices/five-common-misconceptions-
about-dying

Zyga, L. (2011, March 8). *Ecological burial involves freeze-
drying, composting the corpse.* Phys.org.

https://phys.org/news/2011-03-ecological-burial-involves-freeze-drying-composting.html

www.ingramcontent.com/pod-product-compliance
Lightning Source LLC
Chambersburg PA
CBHW051739250726

48659CB00001B/153